# Polymer Clay
# Master Class Series

## Tips, Techniques & Projects For Beginners

Evi Boyle

Content, Photography & Copyright © 2014 Evi Boyle

All rights reserved.

ISBN: 10: 1481811738

ISBN-13: **978-1481811736**

## DEDICATION

This book is dedicated to my lovely husband for putting up with all my crazy ideas

# Contents

| | | |
|---|---|---|
| Introduction | | Page 8 |
| Chapter 1: | Choosing Your Clay | Page 11 |
| | Storing Your Clay | Page 21 |
| Chapter 2: | Working Space, Safety & Tools | Page 23 |
| | Standard Safety | Page 24 |
| | Fumes Safety | Page 25 |
| | Tools | Page 26 |
| | Project 1. Making a Pin Tool | Page 29 |
| Chapter 3: | Getting To Grips With Your Clay | Page 31 |
| | Project 2. Conditioning Your Clay | Page 33 |
| | Project 3. Basic Round Button | Page 35 |
| | Project 4. Basic Triangular Button | Page 37 |
| | Project 5. Basic Square Button | Page 38 |
| | Project 6. Colour Mixing | Page 39 |
| | Project 7. A Monochrome Range | Page 41 |
| | Project 8. Making A Gradient | Page 42 |
| Chapter 4. | Decorative Skins and Canes | Page 43 |
| | Project 9. Bulls Eye | Page 44 |
| | Project 10. Frog Spawn/Cobweb | Page 45 |
| | Project 11. Spiral | Page 48 |
| | Project 12. Stripe / Humbug | Page 50 |
| | Project 13. Checkerboard | Page 52 |
| | Project 14. Checkerboard Skin | Page 54 |
| | Project 15. Checkerboard Bead | Page 56 |
| | Project 16. Plain Backed Pendant | Page 59 |
| | Project 17. Tube Beads | Page 61 |
| | Project 18. Rondelle Beads | Page 65 |
| | Project 19. Recycled Clay Cane | Page 67 |

# Contents

|  |  |  |
|---|---|---|
|  | Project 20. Recycled Pendant Bead | Page 69 |
|  | Project 21. Recycled Pendant Disc | Page 70 |
|  | Project 22. Recycled Pendant Heart | Page 71 |
| Chapter 5. | Fauxing it | Page 73 |
|  | Project 23. Dalmatian Jasper | Page 74 |
|  | Project 24. Turquoise | Page 76 |
|  | Project 25. Burr Walnut | Page 79 |
|  | Stone Recipe Chart | Page 84 |
|  | Project 26. Easy White Granite | Page 85 |
|  | Project 27. Easy Moonstone | Page 87 |
|  | Project 28. Easy Lava Rock | Page 88 |
|  | Project 29. Precious Metals | Page 89 |
|  | Project 30. Foils & Leaf | Page 91 |
| Chapter 6. | Findings | Page 93 |
|  | Glossary of terms | Page 96 |
|  | About the Author | Page 100 |

Authors Note

The best way to use this book is to work through it, but if you're anything like me you'll see something you want to try right away.

The book has been designed to take this into consideration and so the main thing is just have fun.

> The tips and Projects book is designed to start you off and push you forward at a steady working pace. Once you learn, you can create your own wonderful beads, buttons, bracelets, necklaces, the list is limited only by your imagination.

> This is the first book I've ever created, I'm going by my own experience in the hope that you can avoid making my mistakes.

# Introduction

Where do I begin...?
I fell in love with clay over two decades ago and I haven't been able to put it down ever since.
I never get bored because there are so many types of clay on the market and new ones are being brought out every day.
...It just sparks my imagination
I will admit though, when I was starting out I almost gave up, it was one learning curve after another, from the time I overcooked it and had a black smoke in the kitchen for days, to the time I wrapped a piece I'd spent hours on in cling film to keep the dust off.
...I came back a day later to find the clay had eaten the cling film and I was left with a sticky gooey mess.
Silly mistakes on my part, it's been a long path to get here but what can I say other than it has inspired me to write this... The first in a series of books that hopefully ensures you have fun with it a lot faster than I did, avoiding all of my mistakes along the way.

The polymer clay master class series of books are specifically designed around the skill and comfort level of the individuals who use them.

**This is the Techniques and Skills Book for Beginners.**

The aim of every book I produce will be to ease you into various processes that allow you to immediately work at a speed you are comfortable with, pushing you that little bit further with each new page whilst only using the materials and tools you need for the sections you are undertaking.

Projects will also be focused around the skills you have learned in each book; those skills will be transferable to your own future creations.

If you need ideas you'll also see lots of fun examples spread throughout the book that you are more than free to copy.

Polymer clay in particular is fantastic clay for the hobbyist and the professional, because it's clean and easy to use, it's a wonderfully versatile modeling material which can be cooked at home unlike traditional clay.

…And unlike traditional clay it comes in convenient handy sized blocks that resemble 'to my mind anyway' blocks of solid water colour.

…I think of them like this because they're simple to mix, use, and blend, just like paint.

They come in a wide variety of colours.

…Again just like paint, and they're fun no matter what your age is …just like paint.

There is only one slight difference and that is once your project is complete, to harden it you need a basic domestic oven. The clay is cooked at a fairly low temperature for a short time and finally you're finished unless you want to glaze it. As I said earlier there are lots of clays to choose from; you can pick them up easily from your local craft shop, or the internet.

The important thing to remember in cooking it though is always to read the instructions on the back because they all vary slightly from one type to another.

…Saying this clay has to be the first thing we look at because when you start the only tools you really need are your hands, a bit of patience and a good imagination, everything else is just an added bonus so let's get started.

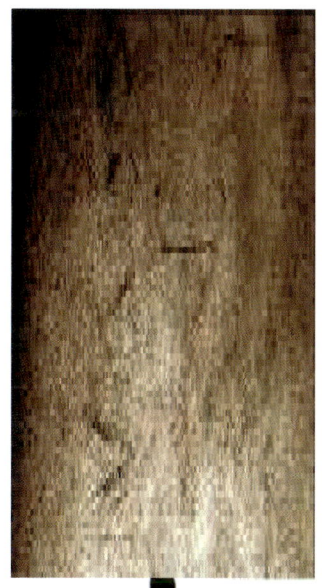

An example what you can do in this book would be these cool charms. You can buy the slip findings and the ball findings online or from any good craft shop. The stars and hearts etc. are created using aspic cutters purchased from your local cook shop.

Find out how to make the decorative canes from page 43 onwards

10

# CHAPTER ONE

# choosing your clay

It's always good to take your time when you're choosing your clay, especially if you've never used it before.

If you buy it over the internet without really seeing it for example you won't know what it's really like just by sight. Grab a block of sculpey super firm, you'll get it home and it will put you off polymer clay for life, it's just so hard to condition and yet it's such a wonderful clay to use for certain things.

There are clays that do have a specific purpose and they are only meant for that purpose, with that in mind the following chapter might seem a bit boring but hopefully it will tell you exactly what each clay does and does not do.

**Clays Featured**
Fimo Classic
Fimo Soft
Fimo Effects
Pastel
Gemstone
Glitter
Glow in the Dark
Transparent
Stone
Metallic
Air Dry
Air Light
Microwave
Natural
Sculpey III
Sculpey Original
Sculpey Granitex
Premo & Premo Accents
Bake N Bend
SuperFlex
Eraser Clay
Bake Shop
Pluffy
Ultra Light
Super Sculpey
Super Sculpey Firm
Super Sculpey Living Doll

Candy Stripe / Humbug beads on page 50.

## Polymer Clay
At the moment there are two main suppliers in this category FIMO & SCULPEY and they produce the following products:

## FIMO Classic
Strong with excellent flexibility, not too soft, this clay is suitable for heavily detailed work; it comes in 24 easily mixable colours.
When baked it can be sanded and drilled after it has cooled.
Drawbacks, none really, though it does take a while to condition and it's probably not suitable for weak, or tiny fingers.

| -0 white | -1 yellow | -15 golden yellow | -4 orange | -2 red | -29 carmine | -23 bordeaux |
|---|---|---|---|---|---|---|
| -21 magenta | -61 violet | -6 lilac | -34 navy blue | -33 ultramarine | -37 blue | -32 turquoise |
| -38 teal | -5 green | -57 leaf green | -43 light flesh | -45 dark flesh | -02 champagne | -17 ochre |
| -74 terracotta | -77 chocolate | -9 black | | | | |

## FIMO Soft
A strong clay, again with excellent flexibility; great for beginners, it comes in 24 easily mixable colours which can be sanded and drilled when cool.
Drawbacks, meant for children this clay can get too soft, it conditions really fast and if you over condition it, it can become sticky to use but fortunately this is easily corrected, aside from this it mixes well with additives and is suitable for everyone.

| -0 white | -10 lemon | -16 sun flower | -42 tangerine | -24 indian red | -26 cherry red | -22 raspberry |
|---|---|---|---|---|---|---|
| -61 purple | -62 lavender | -63 plum | -35 windsor blue | -33 brilliant blue | -37 pacific blue | -39 peppermint |
| -56 emerald | -53 tropical green | -50 apple green | -43 flesh | -70 sahara | -76 cognac | -7 caramel |
| -75 chocolate | -80 dolphin grey | -9 black | | | | |

# FIMO Effects Clay

## Pastel colours

| 105 | 405 | 205 | 605 | 305 | 505 |
|---|---|---|---|---|---|
| vanilla | peach | rosé | lilac | aqua | mint |

## Gemstone

| 206 | 306 |
|---|---|
| rose quartz | ice crystal blue |

## Glitter

| -052 | -112 | -202 | -602 | -302 | -502 | -812 |
|---|---|---|---|---|---|---|
| white | gold | red | purple | blue | green | silver |

| -903 |
|---|
| stardust |

## Glow in the Dark / Night Glow

| -04 |
|---|
| nightglow |

## Translucent

| -014 | -104 | -404 | -204 | -604 | -374 | -504 |
|---|---|---|---|---|---|---|
| translucent | yellow | orange | red | purple | blue | green |

## Stone

| -003 | -803 |
|---|---|
| marble | granite |

## Metallic

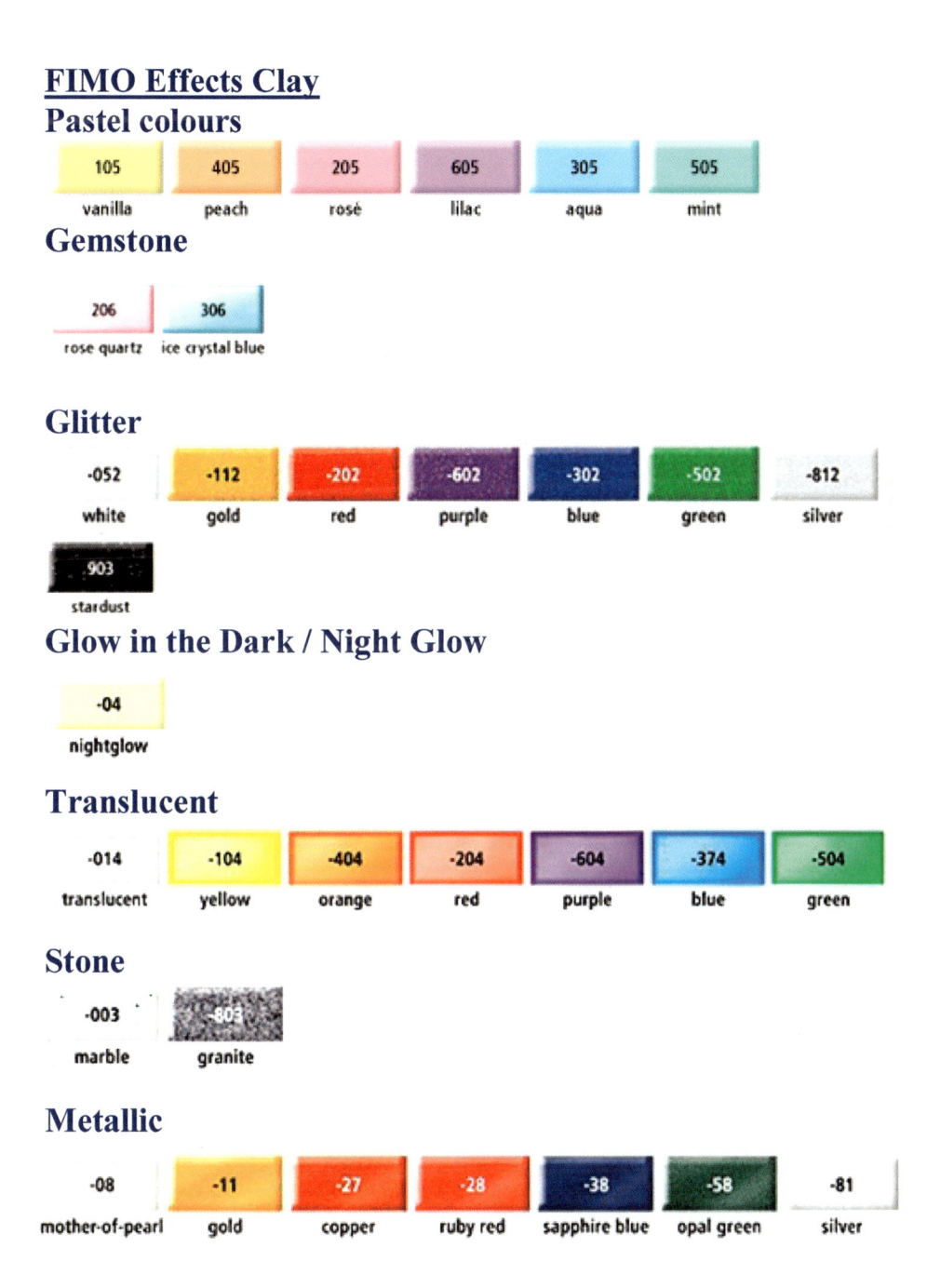

| -08 | -11 | -27 | -28 | -38 | -58 | -81 |
|---|---|---|---|---|---|---|
| mother-of-pearl | gold | copper | ruby red | sapphire blue | opal green | silver |

**FIMO Effect Clays** do what they say on the wrapper; strong soft and easy to use, the Pastel, Gemstone, Night Glow, Glitter, Translucent, Stone and Metallic colours compliment the main range of colours and they mix easily with other brands.

14

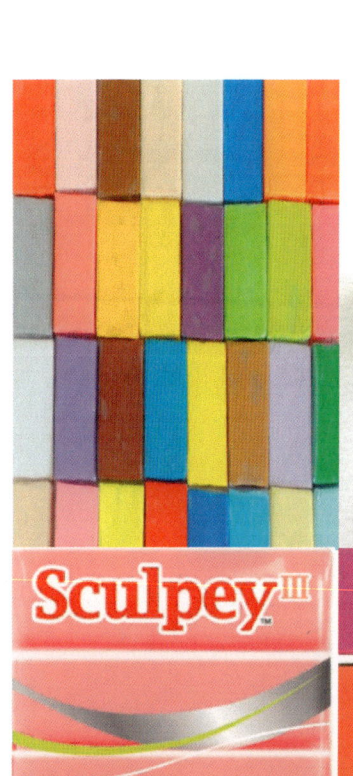

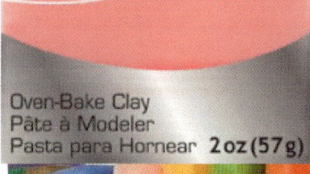

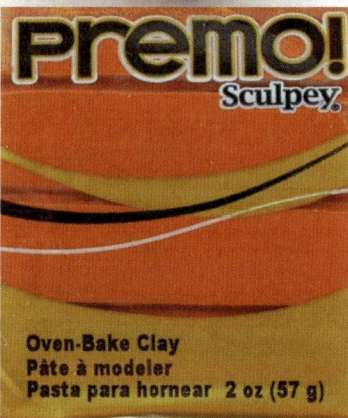

## Other clays that FIMO provides are:

### Basic Air Dry

| -0 | -43 | -76 |
|---|---|---|
| white | flesh | terracotta |

This clay has a soft very natural feel to it; it's very easy to handle, it comes in three colours which can be kept moist with a damp cloth until your project is complete and when you're finished it air dries quickly if the item is small.
It's fantastic for large basic body shapes/sculptures and once dry it can be painted, drawn on, or covered in polymer clay skins for large really colourful projects.
This clay as I said is air dry but you can fire other clays placed on it once it has dried, follow the manufacturer's instruction on the back of each packet for these.
**Hint:** This clay is good to use on its own if you don't have an accurate oven the colours are limited, however you can add food dye to the white clay to make more.

### Air Light

| -0 | -1 | -2 | -3 | -5 | -9 |
|---|---|---|---|---|---|
| white | yellow | red | blue | green | black |

This is what it says it is on the packet with all the properties of Basic Air Dry it's strong and incredibly light, great once again for large objects.
For example masks, or delicate pottery.
**Hint:** if you make decorative dishes for sweets 'or food' of any sort you'll have to seal it because all clays leach in one way or another, and this clay is quite porous like paper when it's dry.

### Microwave

| -0 | -76 |
|---|---|
| white | terracotta |

With all the properties of Basic Air Dry this is also a strong clay and if you don't want to wait overnight for it to harden just pop it in any 600 watt microwave for ten minutes for perfect results.

## Natural

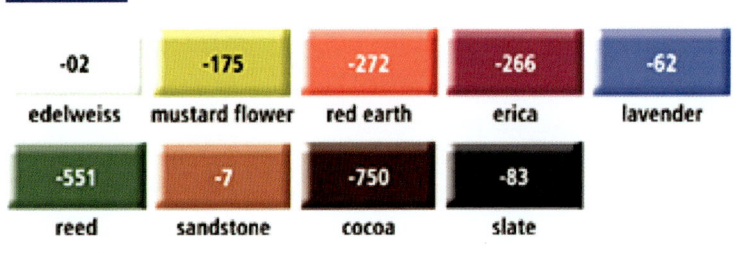

| | | | | |
|---|---|---|---|---|
| -02 | -175 | -272 | -266 | -62 |
| edelweiss | mustard flower | red earth | erica | lavender |
| -551 | -7 | -750 | -83 | |
| reed | sandstone | cocoa | slate | |

Like FIMO Air Dry Basic but made with totally natural ingredients which makes this very safe clay for small fingers.

I've mentioned these clays because although they're not polymer clays they're made by the same people who have expanded the way in which we use all clay as a craft medium today.

These particular clays have a natural affinity to polymer clay and are brilliant when combined in certain projects, especially ones where you need something a little different to work with regarding new textures.

FIMO have thought it through and have done an excellent job at pushing the boundaries and I encourage you to explore them all.

## SCULPEY III

Sculpey III is fantastic clay very like FIMO Soft in its handling capability, it maintains tooling and detailing beautifully and once cured bakes hard and takes on a matte, bisque-type finish.

It comes in 44 stunningly bright colours and is perfect for figurines, cake toppers, beads, chunky jewelry and picture frames etc.

Delicate projects will need some reinforcement.

It is however wonderfully soft clay, especially for the beginner, the colors are some of the most beautiful because they are strong and vibrant. You'll need to reinforce some projects but that is easily done.

Color swatches shown:

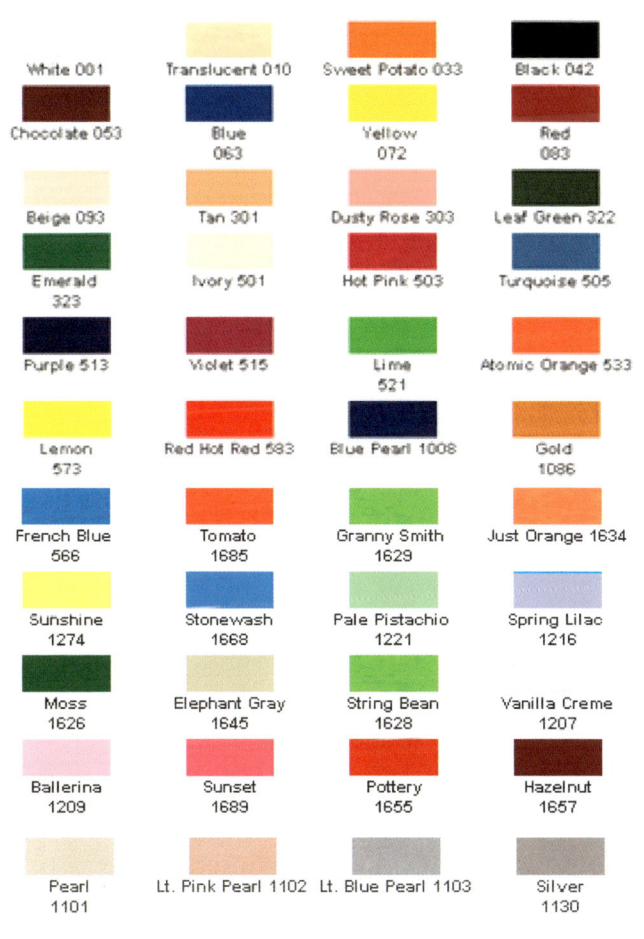

- White 001
- Translucent 010
- Sweet Potato 033
- Black 042
- Chocolate 053
- Blue 063
- Yellow 072
- Red 083
- Beige 093
- Tan 301
- Dusty Rose 303
- Leaf Green 322
- Emerald 323
- Ivory 501
- Hot Pink 503
- Turquoise 505
- Purple 513
- Violet 515
- Lime 521
- Atomic Orange 533
- Lemon 573
- Red Hot Red 583
- Blue Pearl 1008
- Gold 1086
- French Blue 566
- Tomato 1685
- Granny Smith 1629
- Just Orange 1634
- Sunshine 1274
- Stonewash 1668
- Pale Pistachio 1221
- Spring Lilac 1216
- Moss 1626
- Elephant Gray 1645
- String Bean 1628
- Vanilla Creme 1207
- Ballerina 1209
- Sunset 1689
- Pottery 1655
- Hazelnut 1657
- Pearl 1101
- Lt. Pink Pearl 1102
- Lt. Blue Pearl 1103
- Silver 1130

*The bracelets are made using scrap clay and the technique for recycling scrap clay and scrap clay beads are on page 67*

## SCULPEY Original

This is soft and pliable, it works and feels like ceramic clay but will not dry out when exposed to air. After baking, it can be sanded, drilled, carved and painted with water-based acrylic paints or glazed with Sculpey 'or a good quality acrylic' Glaze

## SCULPEY Granitex

If you need clay that looks like stone but don't know how to create a stone effect then this is lovely clay to use, it comes in some very pretty pebble effect colours. It's a very strong little clay and although it's not so good for heavily detailed work (i.e. tooling) it is stunning to look at, and it's great for use in sculptural chunky jewelry and all molded items.

- Brown #3001
- Green #3002
- Orange #3003
- Blue #3004
- Red #3005
- Violet #3006
- Black #3007
- Turquoise #3008

Though Granitex is one of my all-time favorite clays because it is so pretty, it struggles when it comes to detailed work because there is a fabric mix through it, so you need to be patient. On the plus side it is a really strong little clay especially on small thick pieces because of the bound fibers used to create the stone pattern, they act like an internal scaffold.

## Finally Some Other Clay Types and Brands

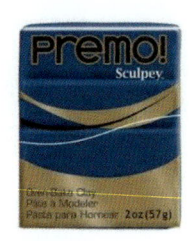

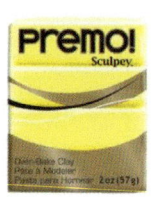

### PREMO & PREMO Accents
After conditioning this clay is soft enough to blend easily but firm enough to hold fine detail, it lends itself well to a variety of specialized techniques, and it's perfect for canes, mokume cane and mica shift. PREMO & PREMO Accents are clays that maintain their flexibility, the finished product remains very strong and this unique characteristic makes it durable clay, ideal for fine jewelry and a variety of functional items we use every day. It comes in 34 densely saturated colours and can be mixed to create custom colors easily making it fantastic for design projects.

## NOVELTY CLAYS

### Glow in the Dark
Wonderfully soft and pliable right from the package, this is standard clay. In the dark it is a ghostly green. I have to mention though that Sculpey also has a selection that glows in a full range of colours.

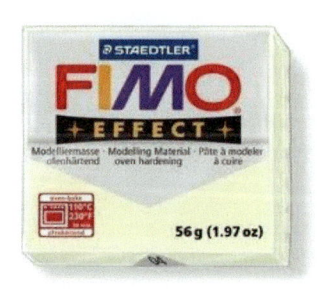

### Bake N Bend
Soft and easy to condition it will not dry out when exposed to air; it stays soft and pliable until baked in a regular oven. Your sculptures will stay rubbery and bendable after baking.

## SuperFlex

Like Bake N Bend this is more for big kids because of its durability and range of craft uses. One of the adult uses is the fact that this clay makes fantastic molds which you can use again and again. If you use it once, it will find a place in your toolbox and you'll wonder how you ever did without it.

## Eraser Clay

It is what it says it is on the packet, Eraser Clay is the polymer clay that becomes a real rubber eraser after it's baked. Great for pencil ends for kids but also wonderful for non- slip mats and decorative coasters.

It comes in similar packaging to Bake N Bend.

## Bake Shop

This is oven-bake clay, soft and easy to condition and perfect for little kids!

The colours can be blended together like Fimo & Sculpey for endless creativity.

This clay does not dry out and stays super soft until you bake it in your home oven.

## Pluffy

Sorry kids again, though I still love it, it's fluffy, squishy, and light and they say it is the most exciting clay launched in years for little fingers.

Even big kids like me can play with it forever though and not get bored PLUFFY never dries out until you cook it.

I use it with my nephew and niece.

## UltraLight

This is lightweight and extremely soft clay, it bakes hard and it won't crack or break, even in larger pieces.

UltraLight also remains flexible when rolled thin so it is ideal for paper crafts.

This is adult clay, or clay for use under some supervision, it dries out really quickly.

### Super Sculpey
This is unique polymer clay, loved by artists, doll makers and animation studios around the world.
It has a ceramic-like feel and is available in semi-translucent beige that, once baked captures the glow of real skin. It can also be mixed with other polymer clays to change the colour.
It's easy to condition right out of the package and stays soft until you bake it and features fine tooling and detailing characteristics, perfect for dolls.

### Super Sculpey Firm
Super Sculpey Firm is the beast, hard to condition but also the answer to a sculptors desire for clay they can carve, tool and sculpt. The extra firm clay is grey in color, making it easy for both sculptors and photographers to see even the tiniest detail and when necessary, catch it on film. After curing in the oven Super Sculpey Firm can be sanded, drilled, carved and painted with water-based acrylic paint. It is by far the most useful clay for precision work, though as I said earlier it is really hard to condition and will give you a work out …but the end result is worth it.

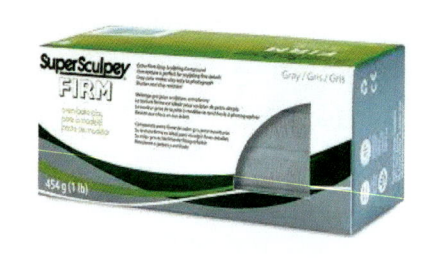

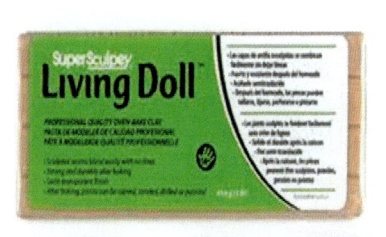

### Super Sculpey Living Doll
Professional quality oven-bake clay specially formulated for doll making. This clay blends easily to make realistic dolls, and it's strong and durable after baking.
Available in 3 popular colors: Beige, Brown and Light.

I'd love to go through them all of the clays I know but the book isn't big enough because more and more are being invented every day. Sorry if this looks like a long winded advertisement for clays but in the first book I'd like you to get to know as many of them as possible.

> **Hint:** If you're using clay for the very first time I suggest Fimo soft in the following colours, red, yellow, blue, black and white. You can choose a pallet which is either Sunflower yellow, Indian red & Windsor blue, or Lemon yellow, Cherry red and Pacific blue. The first is a warm pallet, the second is cold and both sets work well with black and white.

## STORING YOUR CLAY

Polymer clay has a very long life span if you store it correctly. I still have clay I bought years ago, and its fine.

**Tips that keep your clay in great condition:**

- Keep your clay away from direct sunlight, radiators etc.
- Do not store any clay in a plastic container because the clay reacts with the plastic, it melts the container and everything turns into a horrible sticky, gooey, unusable mess.
  'I discovered this the hard way when I first started using polymer clay for the first time.'
- Jam jars are great for storage and they look pretty on a shelf filled with clay.
- If you really have no option other than plastic containers then line them with foil.
- Avoid wood and cardboard boxes, they dry out your clay by leeching out the polymer in it..
- To rescue slightly sticky clay add a light powdering of cornstarch, or talcum powder and roll it as though you were making pastry, this works well on soft clay as well.
- For new really soft clay straight from the packet, either do the above, or roll flat, place between two sheets of paper and leave overnight, this takes a bit of patience but it leaches the polymer out of the clay evenly and leaves you with a firmer working medium the next day.
- Another way to harden soft clay is to pop it in the fridge for an hour or two.
- Keep baby wipes beside you, clean surfaces to ensure your clay doesn't pick up loose dust or grubby finger prints.
- If possible always work on a clean sheet of paper, or even better a white tile, you can get scrap end of line tiles from any good DIY store but if you can't get one any clean flat surface will do.

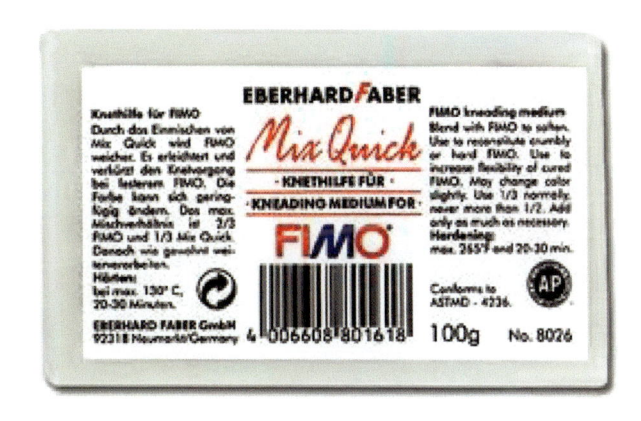

- Long nails are polymer clays worst enemy, they get dirty and they transfer the dirt really easily deep into the clay.
- If your clay gets really marked though and it's on the surface don't worry, you can sand most marks off once cooked with some light sand paper.

- Dark clay, red clay especially seems to be the worst clay on the planet for staining hands; surface and other clays try to keep it away from projects until you need to use it.
- For really, really hard/old clay you can get a softening medium; FIMO does a great one.
  You just crumble up the old clay and add it to it, it takes a little time and again you mix it as though you were making pastry.
  If you don't have access to **FIMO MIXQUICK** just add some over conditioned translucent Sculpey, or really soft clay in the same colour and mix in the same way. Both are good because they don't change the clays color, and you can use them in moderation to get the exact consistency.

- Second tip for really hard clay, place in a resalable freezer bag (I know I said don't use plastic but your clay will only be in the bag for a short period of time) break your clay into tiny bits, seal and drop into 'hand hot' water, your clay will soften quickly and you can condition it from there.

### Liquid Sculpey

Liquid Sculpey is the final clay I will mention in this section, it's great for a variety of things and one of the best is the fact that it is the superglue of the polymer clay world. It's also great for filling in cracks and for image transfer but we'll only be covering some of those uses in this book.

## CHAPTER TWO

# working space, safety & tools

## **Working Space**

You don't need a lot of space for polymer clay, most of the time I work in my converted loft. I have shelves piled with knick knacks that I think will be useful and as I work on lots of different hobbies and projects at once it usually means I'm crammed into a little corner because the others are filled with bits and bobs, I am also a slob as you can see.

…You may laugh but I started off with one block of clay like you, it draws you into lots of other crafts as you'll see in this series of books.

…Don't get me wrong though, for those really special projects I do always tend to work on a clean surface ' a sheet of white paper' on a tray, balanced on my knees, near a good light source, or a cheap sketch pad.

At the end of the day you don't need a lot of space, just a comfortable chair, good light and maybe if you're pushing the boat out, a small table.

…Just make sure the surface you do use isn't used for food preparation and if there is no way around using this space, make sure it has a removable, preferably washable covering.

Once you've found 'your' perfect clay and your perfect working space take some time get used to it, then without realising it you'll start picking up and collecting all sorts of tools.

We're only using a few in this book and I'll show you how to make them soon together with all the other cool things. Regarding tools, if space is 'very' limited a metal toolbox is essential 'because as I mentioned earlier polymer clay dissolves plastic over time' and a large upturned tea tray with cushion attached works well because it means you don't have to spend ages setting up 'and cleaning up' all of the time, which is off putting.

This set up is also good because you can stop mid project and pop the whole lot in a safe place until you're ready to start again.

## Standard Safety

Most polymer clays are fine once they're cooked; you can use them with food for short term exposure items, cake toppers etc. but I have to state again that mixing a chemical based resin with anything to do with food in general is not a good idea at the best of times and though there are lots of voices saying polymer clay is not a toxic substance it's reasonable to say why take a chance.
I keep all of my tools for clay completely separate from food and food preparation areas, and this is a personal choice.
Most popular polymer clays have been tested by the Arts & Crafts Materials Institute (ACMI) before being given the listing of non-toxic, so when you purchase your clay look for the little (ACMI) seal of approval on each packet of clay, and you will see a notification that it conforms to the ASTM D-4236 standard.
Any product with this label is certified to be "properly labelled in a program of toxicological evaluation by a medical expert."
The ASTM D-4236 standard is meant as classification of art materials for adults.

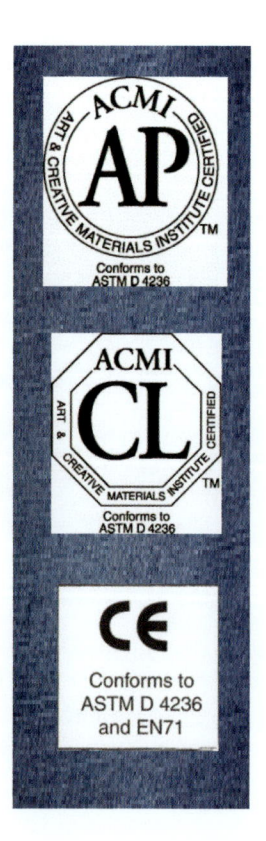

With regards to Health & Safety for children 'since the late 1930's' products are tested under the children's standard and will bear one of two titles. "CP" indicating a certified product undergoing approval and "AP" indicating the product has been approved for use by children.

But in general most clay is safe.

I bet I've confused you now and you're saying if polymer clay is non-toxic and safe why can't you put food in a Polymer Clay bowl...?

The answer is it has a lot more to do with the food than the clay; you see inert baked clay is not going to poison you but at the same time it's still not food grade plastic because it's very porous, and it isn't dishwasher safe either, so you won't be able to clean it well enough to insure there are no bacteria lurking somewhere. We shouldn't assume that all materials that are not food grade must be dangerous either, some pottery, for example, contains lead, and we are happy to cook in it and drink from it. In fact we could go on about the pros and cons and what we mean by food safe and not food safe but at the end of the day polymer clay simply doesn't sanitize well.

The general rule when working with clay, and one I follow is if you feel the need to take precautions in order to feel safe then that's fine but at the very least use common sense, enjoy it and if you use something you shouldn't have like a favorite knife, pop it in the dish washer or give it a good scrub.

# Fumes Safety

Polymer clay is a fantastic fun medium and with regards to the point I made earlier in this book, water colour paints are more dangerous. When you've finally chosen your clay, and you're working space, unwanted fumes really are the only concern you will have to be careful about. As a newbie, you might be tempted to put the heat up, or your oven may be hotter than you think, plus different clays fire at slightly different temperatures so do a very small test piece first, I learned the hard way from experience.

Baking your clay normally will produce a slight smell which tends to go away in around five minutes, if you burn it but that's a different story…

Burnt clay causes fumes and these fumes do have a very nasty smell. Burning clay releases hydrochloride gas which can irritate the mucus membranes and cause stinging to the eyes, nose, and throat so if your clay does burn, turn off the oven, open the windows and leave the area until the gas dissipates.

I have to admit that I burnt my clay the first time I'd used it. My oven was hotter than I expected it to be and my clay burnt 'quite badly' my mascara ran, I stood outside coughing and I looked like COCO the clown which everyone thought was funny except me, but I was too annoyed to care because I'd burnt the beads I was making to a frazzle.

So my rule of thumb is start on a temperature that is 5 degrees lower, keep an eye on it the first time and work up because you can't overcook polymer clay but we'll get to that later.

# Tools

I said earlier that I will only include the tools in this book that I will be using in the projects for the techniques that I will be teaching you, there is nothing worse than buying a lot of fancy stuff then finding out we never used it.

### The Hand Tool

The first and most important tool you will use in this book with your clay is this tool, **the hand tool**, easy to get hold of and you can use it instantly because there is no packaging.

### Good Points:

You will find that it comes in a wide range of sizes but that your hand tool will be perfect for whatever you want to use it for, it is a very adaptable tool and probably the most important tool you will own.

## Bad Points:
If you overwork the hand tool it can get tired, worn out and suffer from a technical glitch known as RSI (Repetitive Strain Injury).

Make sure the hand tool rests well between projects and try to have at least two projects on the go so that you can do simple non exertive tasks between periods of conditioning the clay; finally the hand tool gets dirty very easily.

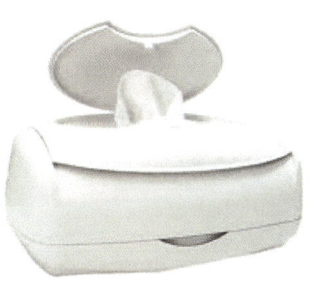

## Care of the Hand Tool
When using polymer clay it is wise to keep a box of baby wipes nearby, your hands pick up everything and transfer it to the clay.

Little specks of dust aren't so bad, but when you've been using dark clay and you move on to a pale clay, or worst of all white, or translucent clay it's sometimes not a pretty sight.

Getting into the habit of using a baby wipe on your hands and the also on the surface you are working on will save you hours of grief.

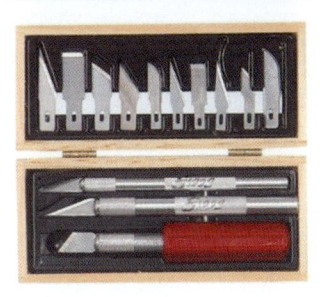

## A Good Craft Knife (with a rounded handle if possible)

This compliments the hand tool in many ways, I have a Stanley knife that I've pinched the blade from as well, and I'll show you that later because I use it instead of the long blade. It saved me around ten pounds and it was a lot easier to get than a clay slicer I can tell you.

Collecting an array of knives is a good thing over time but in this book you only really need two.

If you can get a knife with a rounded handle it doubles up in most instances as a rolling pin and the long blade slices your canes.

When you do start to get a good collection going find a small box to store them in, knives are dangerous in the wrong hands and for some reason it's the first thing little fingers want to pick up.

### Pin Tools
You'll need these to pick up tiny bits of clay and to make holes; once again you can buy the expensive ones or just get a darning needle and make the one I'll show you later in this chapter.

### Homemade Pin Tools
Whatever way you look at it all clay tools are expensive and you should buy them but not right away, it took me years to collect mine.

In the meantime make your own, some of my best tools are home made because they were made for a specific purpose and all you need are a few bits and bobs you'll find lying around and some scrap clay.

A selection of homemade pin tools, you don't have to stop here though, you can make tools out of anything and if you do you'll soon have a fine selection.

**Finally for this section of the book anyway**

### Baby Powder
I hear the purists out there screaming NO…… but come on guys, corn flour, flour, special release powder; it all works as long as you don't go overboard.
…Besides baby powder smells nice and it's good for your skin.

# Project 1. Making A Pin Tool

You will need a selection of pins and nails, younger individuals should use dulled cocktail sticks, or even blunt oven safe plastic needles for safety. Once you have these grab some scrap clay and you're ready to begin.

Form a ball with your scrap clay and then push the blunt end of your cocktail stick / skewer gently into it until the flat edge is almost at the base of the ball. Make sure you squeeze the sides gently when you do this to get a firm bond.

When you're happy that the cocktail stick / skewer has a good tight fit, start to roll the excess clay into a sausage and begin to form the handle. Don't worry if it appears to be too thick you can cut the excess off at the end.

# Project 1. **Cont:**

Once you feel that your handle has reached the right thickness it's time to start pinching the end nearest the point. Roll it until it is rounded and even. If necessary you can trim off any excess at the tip with a sharp knife.

By using scrap clay you'll form a natural pattern without even trying. If however you want handles that are really special I'll be showing you various techniques further into the book as we progress and you can decorate using them.

In the picture opposite you'll see the different ends, a point, an angled end, a flat end and a fat nib end. I just wanted to show you that you can make a tool out of just about anything and I'm sure you'll make some great ones.

## CHAPTER THREE

# getting to grips with your clay

**There is a question that I keep getting asked all of the time and that question is: How do I choose which colour to use first?**
**Answer:** It depends on your personal preferences and what you want to do with it, but if you're using it for the first time I'd say use any colour you want as long as you stick to the same type of clay, if you're using FIMO soft for example make sure it's all FIMO soft.
**When you start you will encounter some of the terms below.**

## The colour wheel

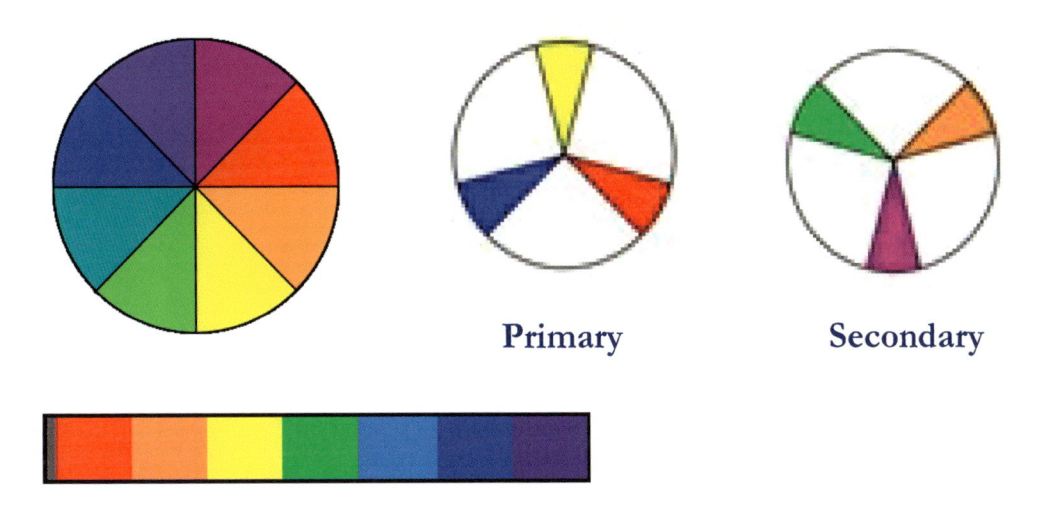

Primary          Secondary

**The chromatic scale** 'above' is made up of red, blue and yellow, these are called **primary** colours. On either side are orange, green, turquoise and purple, these are called **secondary** colours and they are obtained by mixing two of the primary colours together in equal amounts, mix two secondary colours and you get a **tertiary** colour and so on.

**The achromatic scale** starts with pure white, it proceeds through various shades of grey (usually 10%) and ends in jet black..

**The monochromatic scale** also starts with white and progresses steadily through various shades of the same colour (usually 10%) until it finishes at the colours most saturated state.

Finally, as far as your beginners lesson is concerned:

**Analogous,** a group of colours that are adjacent to each other on the color wheel, one will be a dominant primary colour, or secondary colour, with two on either side enhancing it, these tend to be tertiary.

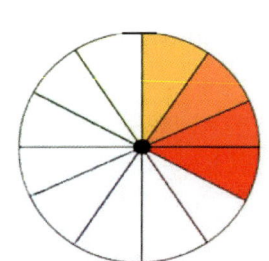

**Complimentary,** two colours directly opposite one another on the colour wheel. They form the black and white of the colour world because they always clash (in a nice way) and they are a great colour choice for statement pieces.

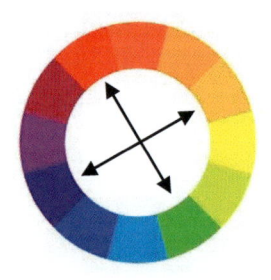

At the end of the day your artwork will come down to contrast if you want it to be striking, or subtle it will be the colours you choose.
For instance the most striking colour scheme is often in black and white, or any direct complimentary scheme.
The most subtle work is often light grey and white, or analogous.
Try different combinations because the same design can look completely different when it is created in a different colour scheme.

# Project 2. **Conditioning Your Clay**

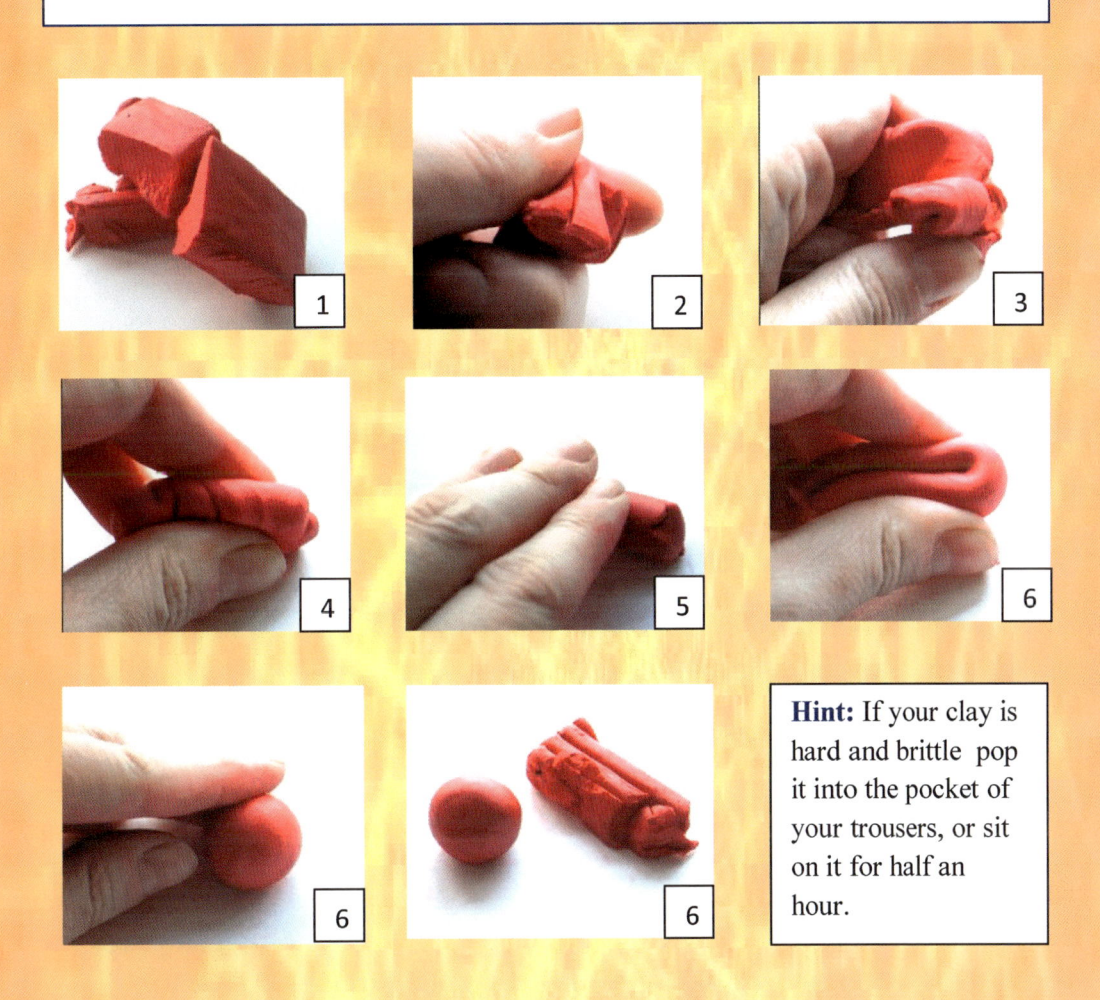

**Hint:** If your clay is hard and brittle pop it into the pocket of your trousers, or sit on it for half an hour.

No 1. Choose your clay.　No 2. Warm they clay in your hand.
No 3. Squeeze it.　　　　No 4. Fold it.
No 5. Roll it.　　　　　　No 6. Repeat from beginning

Carry out the above steps until the clay feels soft and forms a malleable ball. I should add at this stage some clays take a while but when the steps are complete and the clay is soft you'll be ready to start having some serious creativity and fun.

### What is conditioning you ask?
Answer: Conditioning is the process that prepares your clay; it is done by working, kneading the clay with your hand like dough until it reaches a good working consistency. The warmth of your hand, pressure and compression will change the texture of the clay making it softer and more pliable.

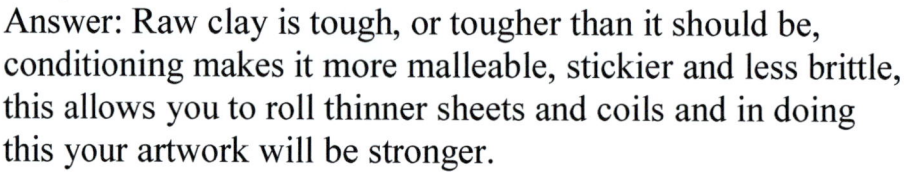

### Why do I need to do this?
Answer: Raw clay is tough, or tougher than it should be, conditioning makes it more malleable, stickier and less brittle, this allows you to roll thinner sheets and coils and in doing this your artwork will be stronger.

**Tip:** Even if clay is soft straight from the packet you should still condition it, and then add a little powder.

### Question: Is there a way to speed up this process?
Answer: There are a few, which are good for anyone with hands that are not strong, or like me arthritis sufferers. Working with clay is great exercise but if you have a lot of clay that you want to condition it can get tiring.

### Pre warming clay.
Put the clay in a warm place for half an hour, I sit on mine while I watch television, or put it in my back pocket.

Some people use a hot water bottle or put it on a radiator you have to be careful if you do this because your clay can start cooking.

Some people use a food processor, they keep it especially for their clay and it's great because the friction from the blades chops and warms the clay.

If you do get a food processor blend the clay in short bursts of 10 seconds. If you don't have a food processor chop it with a knife into little bits, pop in a bag and sit on it, trust me it works.

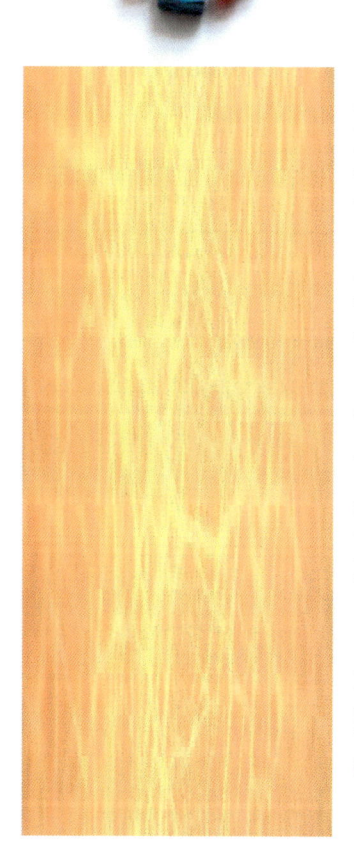

# Project 3. Basic Round Button

Condition three balls of clay and then set them to one side, you will only be using one colour at any given time in this project, so the choice of clay and the colours that you do use are completely up to you.

Take the first ball of clay and flatten it into a disc which should be no thinner than 5mm, because we want this to be a sturdy little button. Later when you start making your own you'll be able to set the thickness you want.

This is slightly bigger than normal but practicing on a button this size will get you used to the various techniques involved in making them, such as rolling them along their edge to get a clean line on your finished piece.

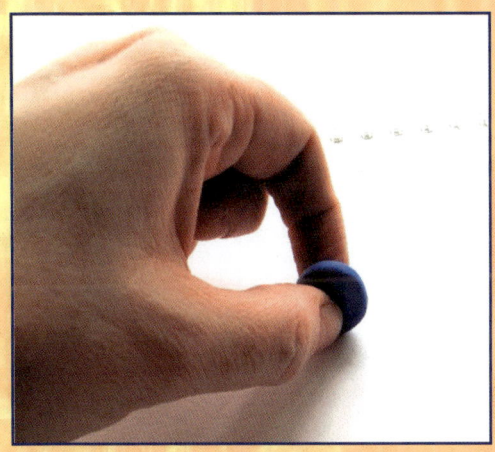

# Project 3. Basic Round Button Cont:

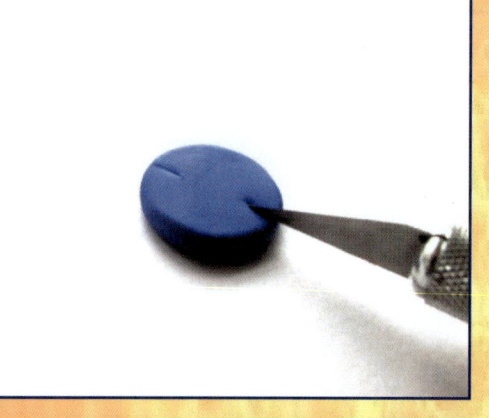

When your button is round and even, lay it on a clean flat surface, take the back edge of your craft knife and press gently, turn the button around 180 degrees and repeat the process on the other side matching up the marks.

Turn the disc again and using the first two marks as guides repeat the process making sure that they are evenly spaced. When your pattern is complete take your pin tool and push downward gently to form the button hole, and repeat.

This is the simplest way to decorate your first button, you can use any of your pin tools as well as your craft knife. In fact you can decorate the button any way you want once you get the hang of it with any of the techniques.

# Project 4. **Basic Triangular Button**

Repeat the process used in button one to form your clay into a 5mm pancake.
From there gently press the edge against a flat surface and pull the sides at the base to form a point, turn and repeat the action to form three sides.

You will now have a flat triangular pancake which is ready for the decoration of your choice. For this button I have used the back of the knife again, even spaced from each edge to form a natural inner triangle.

I've finished it with a few more knife strokes and in this instance I have given it three button holes. You can have as many button holes as you want. Many people feel that you are only allowed two but they're your buttons.

# Project 5. Basic Square Button

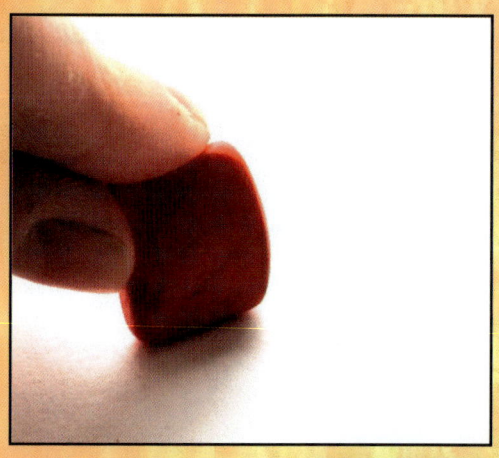

When your button is round and even, lay it on a clean flat surface, take the back edge of your craft knife and press gently, turn the button around 180 degrees and repeat the process on the other side matching up the marks.

Turn the disc again and using the first two marks as guides repeat the process making sure the marks are evenly spaced. When your pattern is complete take your pin tool and push downward gently to form the button hole, and repeat.

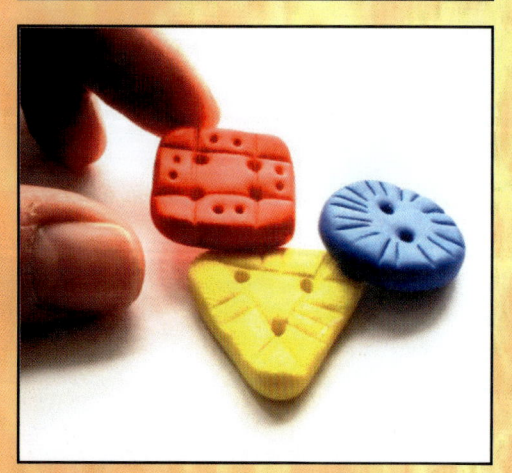

This is the simplest way to decorate your first button. You're saying what have buttons got to do with beads. Well you've chosen clay, you've made shapes and you've drilled basic holes, so I'd say they were a good start.

# Project 6. **Colour Mixing**

Take your raw clay, choose two colours, one should be dark and one should be light. I've taken red and white stone effect because I like them, however blue and white, and black and white are also a good combination.

Make sure clay is well conditioned (see P.30) and when it is roll the first colour into a long log. Set it to one side and roll second into a similar log, when you've done that slice the second log into four equal parts.

Press the first piece of clay into your main log and squish it in thoroughly until it is completely mixed into the main body of the clay. You'll see the colour start to change slightly almost immediately in fact in your hand.

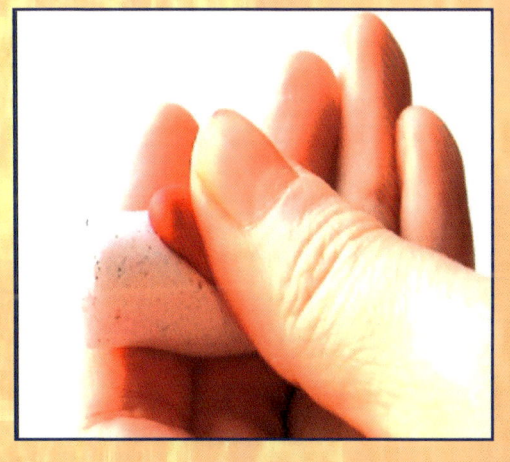

# Project 6. **Colour Mixing Cont:**

When this happens add the second piece and continue in the same vein as the first until all four pieces are mixed into the main piece, or 'more importantly' when you finally reach a colour that you really like.

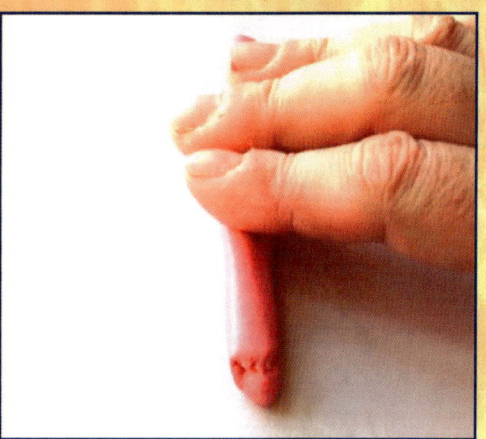

At this stage roll the clay out into a thin log and check the colour is consistent, if you see flecks, or veins as you roll it out, it needs more work. When this happens squish it and roll it a few more times until all the veins and flecks disappear.

When you have finished and the clay is thoroughly mixed, place it between the first two colours and you'll see that a completely new colour has been created. By doing this you can mix the exact colours you'll need for any project.

# Project 7. Monochromatic Colour

Take equal amounts of clay in the colours that you have just made.

Cut each of the blocks into four equal pieces and set out as shown in the picture and diagram.

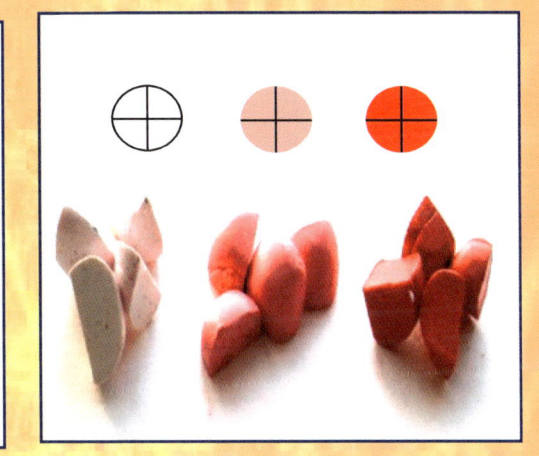

Now make sure that they are set in the groups shown in the image opposite.
The coloured dots above the clay show the quantities, group them in these quantities and you will be ready to start mixing them.

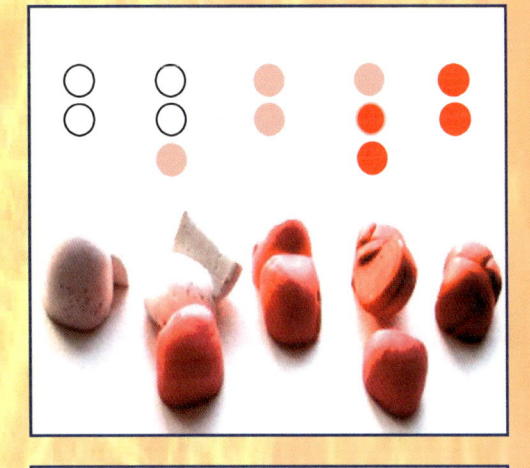

Take each group of clay, carefully mix it in the way you mixed the colours in the previous project, a step at a time. Squish it, then roll it to check the consistency of colour and when you're happy set it to one side.

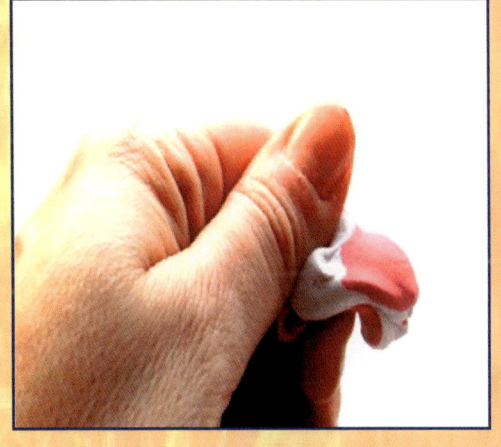

# Project 8. **Graduated Colour**

If you mix up the colours above, in the quantities above, you will end up with five colours that vary slightly, These colours are called monochromatic colours because they all come from the same family range.

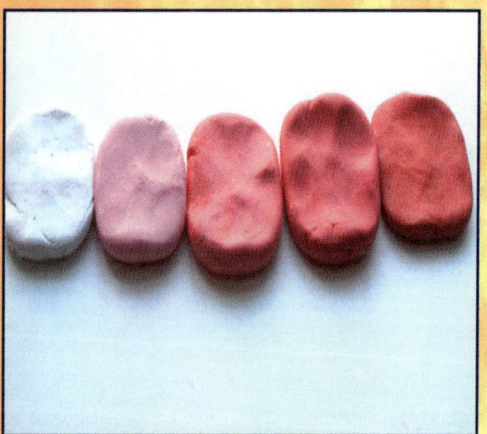

The difference becomes even clearer when you press them into a flat pancake shape and set them side by side.
Make five pancakes as shown opposite and try to keep them even in shape and in thickness as shown.

Place the pancakes in order, starting with the lightest shade through to the darkest.
Press down on them gently and if you slice through with a knife you will make what we term in the world of colour as a gradient scheme.

## CHAPTER FOUR

# decorative skins and canes

Mixing colour is fun and very therapeutic but the next question is what do you do with it after that, you could make little sculptures, or beads, but if you've bought this book I suspect you want to know more than how to do that.

In this section of the book you'll learn how to make pattern canes, from those canes we can make pattered skins which in turn can transform into buttons, pendants, beads and a whole raft of other items

# Project 9. **Bullseye**

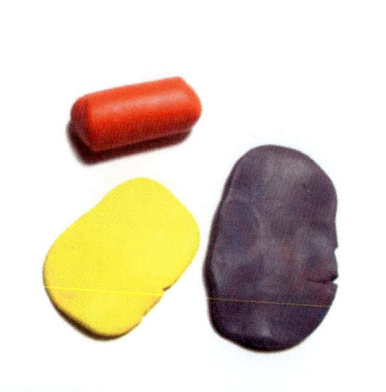

Take 2, or three colours, roll one of them into a basic log and flatten the others into pancakes which are wide enough to wrap neatly around the log. Try to keep relatively the same thickness on each pancake.

Wrap the first layer carefully around the log ensuring that both ends meet. Roll it gently backwards and forwards to seal the join.
At this stage your clay will look a bit like it's covered in a blanket.

Wrap the third colour around, or if your just using two colours repeat the first one again, you can add as many layers as you want to. The more you do add the more complicated your finished pattern will be.

# Project 10. Frog Spawn / Cobweb

Take some black clay roll it into a log and after this is done take a similar amount of white clay and press it into a large enough pancake to surround the black log you just created.
Now wrap it around your log.

Once you have completely covered the log, roll it gently to seal the edge in the way shown opposite.
You now have a basic cane, try to keep it quite thick at this stage and pay particular attention to the seam.

You could use your cane at this stage as it is but if you want to make something more complicated slice your log carefully into two pieces of equal length. Set one of the pieces you have cut to the side for use later.

# Project 10. Frog Spawn / Cobweb Cont:

Roll the second part of the log out evenly with your fingers until it is twice the length of the first log. Slice it, set one half to the side again and repeat. By doing this you will have the pieces to make a frog spawn / cobweb cane.

Cut all of the canes that you've worked on in two, and randomly set some of the pieces to the side in the same way you did with the first ones. Roll the remaining canes to twice their length until you have a collection of widths.

Bunch some of them together carefully and trim. Cut your canes so that they are all the same length you will see the pattern of your cobweb / frog spawn cane form, at this stage add more by gently pressing them all together.

# Project 10. Frog Spawn / Cobweb Cont:

It works best if the pattern is erratic and in no particular order, to do this I just make a load and grab a handful. Once your group is complete and your happy with it squeeze it gently and start to ensure the edges are uniform.

Roll it carefully, try to make sure that the inside of the log remains crisp and clear, if you push the cane too hard the pattern will mush together and all your work will be wasted. So take your time at the bunching stage.

Form a roll and now you should only be tidying up the edge. When this is even leave the cane to settle for at least half an hour, then you can take a sharp craft knife and start to slice it gently, you'll use these later to make skins.

# Project 11. Spiral

Take two equal amounts of clay in the colours of your choice, I chose black and white they're easy to see. Condition and then roll them into flat logs, roughly form rectangular pancakes as shown opposite.

Place one of the rectangular pancakes on top of the other, press it down gently and evenly with your thumb so that both of them bond together neatly, try to keep the rectangular shape as you do this.

Take any tool with a round handle. R roll it gently but firmly at one end of the rectangular pancake until your cane tapers to a fine edge. At this stage take your knife and clean the edge carefully if it isn't straight.

# Project 11. Spiral Cont:

Roll the clean edge of the clay pancake over on itself and carefully fold along the length of the cane. This is the most important part of the spiral cane and if you take your time getting it right then the rest is easy.

Once the whole edge is folded over on itself run it back towards you gently, and almost immediately you will see the pattern in the cane start to form. If the end is messy don't worry just like the edge you can clean that up later.

Leave your cane to settle for at least half an hour, then slice off the edge. The longer you make the rectangular strips at the start of the process the more spirals you will get. You can also use more than two colours of clay.

# Project 12. Stripe / Humbug

Take equal amounts of two colours, I've used black and white again because they're easy to see. Condition them both and then flatten into a square pancake in the same way you did for the spiral cane.

Once again carefully place one colour on top of the other. It is important to check at this stage that they are almost the same thickness as one another, and equally important that you use the same type of clay for both colours.

For example if you use fimo soft with fimo classic your cane will not reduce evenly. To reduce your cane, roll over it carefully and evenly with any round handled tool, or pen, turn over and repeat on the other side

# Project 12. Stripe / Humbug Cont:

Slice it in half, place one half on top of the other.
Press down gently in the way that you did with the first two colours to ensure a good bond. Roll over it again with your round handled tool and slice it in half again.

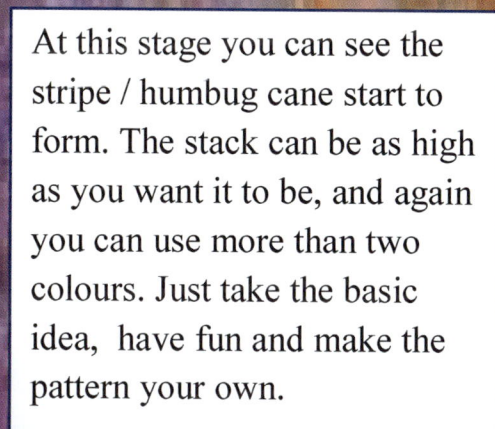

At this stage you can see the stripe / humbug cane start to form. The stack can be as high as you want it to be, and again you can use more than two colours. Just take the basic idea, have fun and make the pattern your own.

This is a strip / humbug cane made with black, white and the monochromatic selection of colour that you made in an earlier exercise. At the end of the day it makes a very pretty uniform cane suitable for lots of projects.

# Project 13. **Checkerboard**

The strip / humbug cane is the start of the checkerboard cane. I've stopped at four layers but as you get better you can go up to around eight layers comfortably as long as you keep them all at the same thickness.

Carefully trim your cane and cut it into 5mm slices. Get as many slices as you can, though you should aim for as many slices as there are layers in you cane because when you put it all back together you'll need to have a square again .

Re stack them (in this case) the white is always over the black as shown in picture opposite. Colours should never rejoin to become a fluid line in a checkerboard cane, if they do take out, or trim the offending slice.

# Project 13. Checkerboard Cont:

In the finished stack, the edge on either side will be really untidy, this is NOT a problem, an untidy edge is good. Take your time and have one last look at the pattern from the front, if you're happy then you're ready to move forward.

Press the cane gently between your fingers, the external pattern will distort slightly, again this is not a problem, your only really interested in the center of the cane. You'll be trimming all of the outer edges later.

Set the cane to one side for around half an hour, after that you can do a test slice, this serves two purposes, it lets you see the inner patter and it also cleans up one of the edges of your cane. If you're happy tidy the rest up.

# Project 14. **Checkerboard Skin**

Take your finished checkerboard cane and start to slice it, the best way to do this is to set it in front of you so that your facing it.
When you're ready take a long blade and bring it down in one smooth action.

You're looking to get as many slice as possible from every cane, because the more slices you can get the bigger the skin and the item you can make with them all. I lightly dip my blade in baby powder which helps it slide through easily.

Take some old scrap clay, condition it until the colour becomes uniform. The finished colours will depend on the scraps used so if you want a light base be sure to use light scraps of clay and leave out any dark ones.

# Project 14. Checkerboard Skin Cont:

Taking the tip of your craft knife gently pick up the first slice and place it on the flat clay scrap, lift the second piece and place it next to the first. At this stage try to keep them all the same way up, it can be difficult.

When you have completely covered your piece of scrap clay, or when you've ran out of slices, whichever comes first, take a round handled tool and gently roll it over everything until the edges start to disappear..

The checkerboard cane is sometimes called a tesserae cane because it looks like the tiny little pieces that they use in mosaics. The bigger the squares the easier the cane is to make, the smaller squares make lovelier patterns though.

# Project 15. **Checkerboard Bead**

Cut your slices in the same way as you did before ensuring that you have enough to cover the bead, plus one for patching up any holes. Use thin slices again because then you can make lots and lots of beads.

Start by wrapping the slices around the center of you bead, take your time and it doesn't matter if the slice overlaps at the end, at least not with this pattern anyway. When you have done this roll it around gently to seal the edges.

If the squares are large enough you should be able to finish with just one piece at the top and one piece at the base. Make sure that you run the lines in the same direction when you add them or your bead will look strange.

An example of beads made by mixing spiral cane and a stripe / humbug canes.

An example of beads made by mixing a cobweb and a recycled canes .

Simple stripe / humbug canes in a range of different colours with yellow as the main one.

# Project 15. Checkerboard Bead Cont:

Your checkerboard bead can be turned into a stunning necklace, or bracelet, just like the ones I've shown you in a few simple steps once you've finished creating it. Roll it around on a flat surface one last time.

Take a pin and dip it into some talc, push it gently downwards into the soft clay and when you feel it hit your work surface, tilt the bead and move the pin backwards and forwards gently, turn it, now repeat from the other side.

The easiest bracelets to make are ones that are threaded with elastic which you can buy online, or from any good craft shop. If you want something a little more special then flick to the back of this book and see my section on findings.

# Project 16. **Plain Backed Pendant**

If you use recycled clay you will have no control over the back of your pendant. This is fine if you intend to skin both sides, or if you like the colour that you came up with when you mixed all of your scraps together.

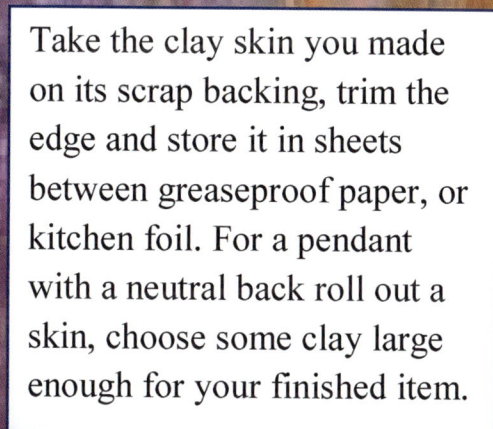

Take the clay skin you made on its scrap backing, trim the edge and store it in sheets between greaseproof paper, or kitchen foil. For a pendant with a neutral back roll out a skin, choose some clay large enough for your finished item.

Place the skin on top of the new clay after you have molded it roughly into shape, and check that it fits with a little overlapping at the edges. You will trim this off later when you tidy it all up before cooking.

# Project 16. **Plain Backed Pendant Cont:**

Hint: If you pop the skin into the fridge for a few minutes, whilst at the same time kneading and heating the new clay the skin will just sink gently into the new clay with a little pressure from your round handled knife.

Trim the edge of the clay, preferably with a long blade. You should do this in the same way you slice a cane 'in one stroke' from above, down to the working surface. You can also use a cookie or an aspic cutter.

Your pendant can be any shape, or form, it doesn't have to be a square or a rectangle. **Hint** if you don't know what you want the shape to be, cut it out in paper first, it'll save you wasting the clay skin you've spent time on.

# Project 17. **Tube Beads**

Take the scrap clay from a skin project and chop it up roughly until you have a little pile. Once you've done this squeeze it all firmly together in order to bind it. Do not mix it at this stage just bundle it together.

Pull the little bundle and press it, as I said before try NOT to roll it at this stage. It doesn't matter if it breaks just put one piece on top of the other and continue the process until you start to see fine lines appear through the clay.

This is a basic marbling technique. At this stage fold the clay over on itself and roll it gently into a long thick log. This will be the center of your tube bead so make sure you have enough of it for your whole project.

# Project 17. **Tube Beads Cont:**

Set the log to one side and then trim a clay skin that you've made earlier so that it will fit comfortably around the main body of the log. The ends don't matter if they stick out slightly, or if they are messy.

Take the log, place the clay skin against it and run your finger along the first edge to help bond the two pieces. When this is done wrap the rest of the skin around the center log carefully until the edges meet.

If your edge is too long you can trim it with a long blade. If your edges fall short, pull the skin gently and tease it filling any gaps. You can do this by taking them and pushing them together with the tips of your fingers.

# Project 17. Tube Beads Cont:

Roll the log gently on a flat surface until the seam disappears, try to keep the main body of the log thick so that your beads are strong. Once you're comfortable you'll be able to make finer beads later

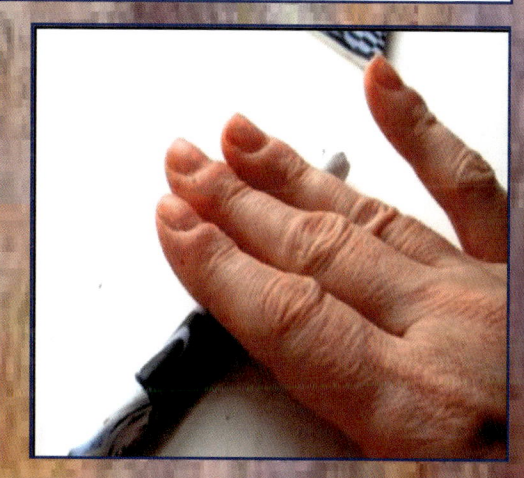

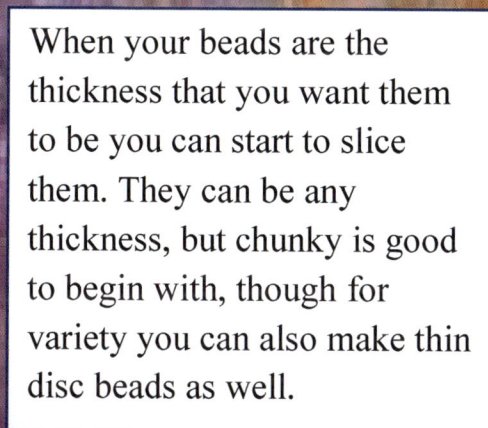

When your beads are the thickness that you want them to be you can start to slice them. They can be any thickness, but chunky is good to begin with, though for variety you can also make thin disc beads as well.

The picture opposite shows short tube beads which I call half in halves. The good thing about these is the fact that you can put the holes for threading anywhere on them. Top to bottom, through the middle, mix and match.

# Project 17. Tube Beads Cont:

Leave your beads for half an hour to settle then take your needle, dip it in some talc, it helps the needle slide back out more easily and the hole is neater. When you've done that turn and do the same from the other side.

The finished beads in this picture have holes that run in various directions, stripe, cobweb and marble techniques are also used.

# Project 18. Rondelle Beads

Repeat the steps used in the previous exercise for your tube beads until you get to this stage. The skin isn't important so choose one you'd like to use in a finished project.
Hint: Cut off a few slices to mix and match later

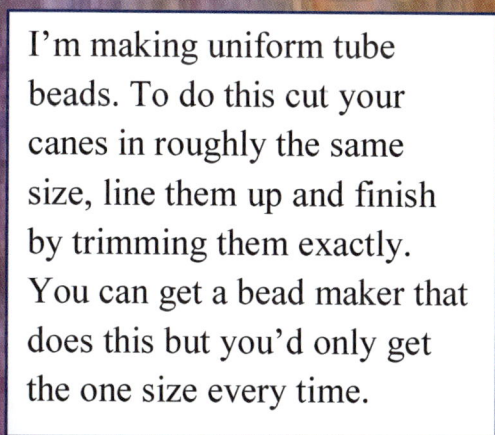

I'm making uniform tube beads. To do this cut your canes in roughly the same size, line them up and finish by trimming them exactly. You can get a bead maker that does this but you'd only get the one size every time.

Take your bead and gently push your pin tool, or a length of rigid wire that has been dipped in talc through it until you can just about see it at the other end. Take it out and repeat from other end to tidy the hole.

# Project 18. Rondelle Beads Cont:

Keeping the edge of the bead near the base of the pin tool, or wire, roll it gently to blunt the edge of the tube. A good way to do this is to get a piece of A4 paper and roll it gently from one end to the other in a straight line.

If the action is jittery, or sticky, simply remove the bead and dip the wire / pin tool into more talc to make the action fluid. When the end of your rondelle is even, see picture opposite, turn your bead and repeat on other side.

You will now have a lovely selection of beads that mix and match perfectly with one another for any project, especially if your if your colour selection is precise and in a specific range, or if it is limited by the clay you use.

# Project 19. **Recycled Clay Cane**

I store all offcuts from my recycled clay in jam jars because there is no such thing as waste clay. When I have enough I empty them all out and chose some to make a recycled cane do it in large chunks for fun patterns.

Squeeze the pieces that you've chosen tightly to bind them, they'll already have been conditioned so your just pulling them together at this stage. Don't squeeze too tightly though you want to keep the patterns.

Whilst still squeezing, form a rough log shape and then roll it gently backwards and forwards to make your cane. It is important to use the log as little as possible at this stage because you actually want the hap-hazard effect.

# Project 19. Recycled Clay Cane Cont:

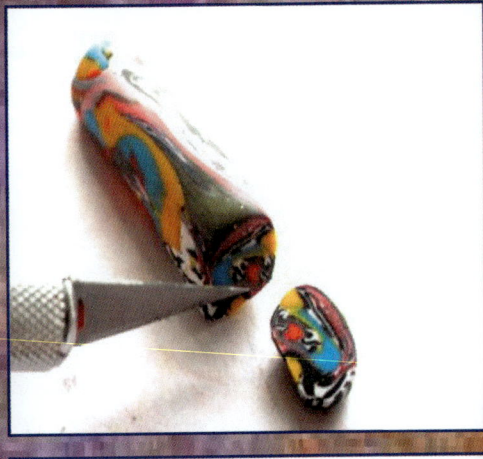

Let the cane settle for half an hour and then slice off the end. At this point you'll see the pattern that the clay jumble created for the very first time. Make sure your recycled cane is large enough for your project at this stage.

You can never re-create a recycled clay cane twice in a row, you will have no control over where the scrap pieces fall and that is where the fun lies because every time you cut it for the first time you never know what you'll get.

If your offcuts are large the cane will be unique but your slices will be uniform within it and that is just another quirk of the recycled cane.
You can have a seriously complicated patterns with little or no effort at all.

# Project 20. Recycled Clay Pendant Bead

The pendant bead is 3 to 4 times the size of a normal bead and you make it when you want to run the pattern uniformly over the whole surface area and not just the front, or the back in the way in which you'd have with a skin.

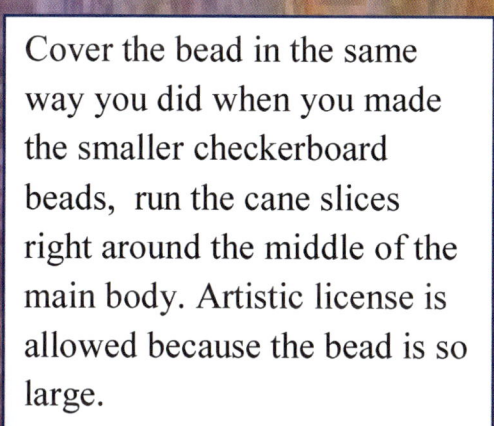

Cover the bead in the same way you did when you made the smaller checkerboard beads, run the cane slices right around the middle of the main body. Artistic license is allowed because the bead is so large.

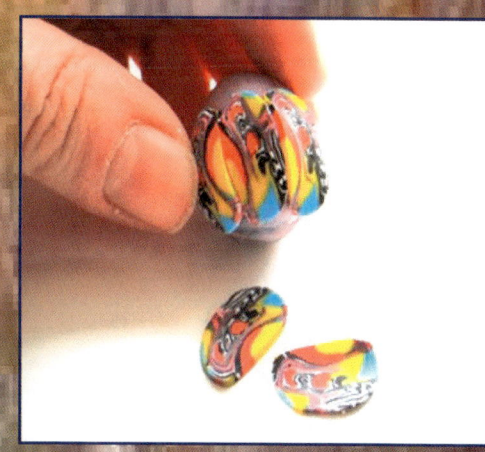

Your finished bead will look roughly like this when it's fully covered.
Check it over, if there are any holes at all fill them in with some offcuts at this stage.
Move on when your happy the bead is covered completely.

# Project 21. **Recycled Clay Pendant Disc**

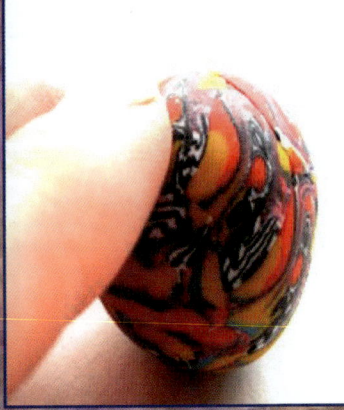

To smooth the bead roll it around your work surface gently until all of the seams join together and your left with an even surface.
Finish by rolling it in both hands because the heat will make the surface smoother.

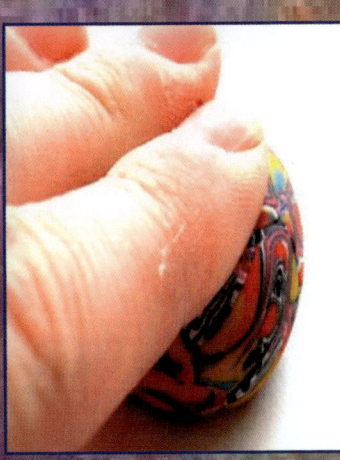

Take your time on the seams, when you are happy that they are finally gone press gently down on your bead, turn it 90 degrees, repeat, turn it again and keep doing this until a disc is formed then run any round handled tool over it

Finish by tilting the bead over on its edge slightly, do this in the same way in which you made the rondelle beads earlier. Run it along your work surface and you will get a beveled edge as shown in the picture opposite.

# Project 22. Recycled Clay Pendant Heart

To turn a disc into a heart is simple. Take your finished disc and pinch one end of it gently between both fingers until you form a point. Place the piece on to your flat work surface and run over it gently with any round handled tool.

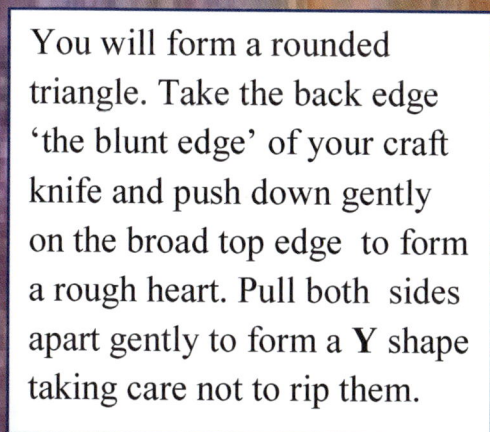

You will form a rounded triangle. Take the back edge 'the blunt edge' of your craft knife and push down gently on the broad top edge to form a rough heart. Pull both sides apart gently to form a **Y** shape taking care not to rip them.

Your heart is almost formed, use your fingers in the same way you used your work surface earlier to tidy up the beveled edge. Put it flat and run them over it gently again and again in a smoothing action as shown.

# Project 22. **Recycled Clay Pendant Heart:**

Finish by rolling over it with any round handled tool. Turn your heart over and if necessary repeat the action on the other side until the heart is smooth and you are happy with the result. Finish by pinching the end of the heart.

When you are done your finished heart will look like this. I have shown you this process in four steps but you can stop at any time using the rough bead, the smooth bead, the disc, or the finished heart as shown.

I call these all-rounders, they are a great way to use up any recycled clay, both within and on the outside of the bead / heart. They are easy to make, look stunning every time, and you can turn them into so many different things.

## CHAPTER FIVE

# fauxing it

To faux it means to fake it, and polymer clay was invented to fake almost anything you want within reason. Hard wood, soft wood, precious metal, semi-precious stones, ceramics, glass, nothing is impossible to copy if you have the patience and a little instruction. I'm touching on stone, wood and metal in this book but I promise to go into everything more thoroughly in other books that I'm in the process of writing with various detailed projects, so think of this as a jump start. Plus I did promise at the beginning you'd only need clay, a few tools and your hands and some faux techniques do involve you buying a few other bits and bobs that you don't need at this stage.

…Also don't forget Fimo and Sculpey do a lovely range of metallic and semi-precious stone effect clay already but if you do want to go that little bit further I recommend these….

# Project 23. **Dalmatian Jasper**

I've chosen this because if you've done all of the projects in black and white like me you have lots of black and white scrap clay. Collect it all together in no real order and make a neat little pile, pressing it together gently.

Next chop it in the same way that you would chop fine onions, don't make the pieces too small. The reason Dalmatian Jasper is so easy to make is the fact that the pattern is erratic and uneven in both size and shape.

This is is a semi-precious stone that designs itself. When the pieces are ready bunch them up, squeeze and roll them gently into a log / cane. Make sure you have enough and also a little spare for earings etc.

# Project 23. Dalmatian Jasper Cont:

The log / cane should still look slightly rough, try not to roll out all of the creases at this stage. Leave it to settle for a few minutes then taking a sharp blade score the top to measure and count the beads that the log will deliver.

When you have done this, dip the blade in some talc and cut each slice in one smooth motion as shown on the picture opposite. Take them pieces and set them to one side so that they don't get damaged as you make more.

The beads can be left as rough beads or they can be rolled to make smooth rondelle, pearl, or tube beads. Set them out in a line laying them in the order you want them to be in the necklace or the bracelet when it's finished.

# Project 24. **Turquoise**

This is easy turquoise. Take some turquoise clay and some black, you could also add a little ultramarine and some cadmium yellow, but for now we'll keep things simple because it's the technique that I really want to show you.

Take both colours and condition them really well. Set them aside until you cut the other colours then chop them up. Chop them roughly at this time, just like Jasper the one thing we **don't** want is small even pieces,

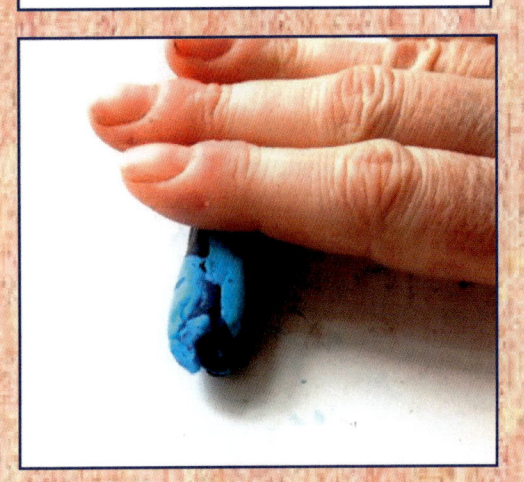

Take all your bits and gently squeeze them together in a rough ball at first. When the ball is tight start to roll it into a thick cane.
Hint if the cane gets too thin you can carefully fold it over once and roll it out again.

# Project 24. Turquoise Cont:

Your finished turquoise will look like this. Leave it to settle for about half an hour then start to tidy it and form beads. The strip made should be a little longer than the bracelet / necklace, and you'll have enough for your project.

In this exercise we're making square turquoise beads.
In order to do this take the cane, flatten it carefully. Slice off either end and take a long blade craft knife, dip it in some talc and in one even stroke push downwards.

By trimming the cane you will see the turquoise pattern start to show itself more clearly. There are many types of turquoise, the one on this page is a stripe variety, it makes fantastic beads and pendants because of the strong pattern.

# Project 24. **Turquoise Cont:**

There will be offcuts, there always are when you faux anything, you can choose to discard these or you can do what I do. I collect all the bits and carefully roll them into a second finer log. Try to keep handling as limited possible.

These rolls make fantastic spacer beads. Roll the log out to the thickness of your largest bead, then taking time mark them by gently pressing with the back of your knife . When satisfied you have enough cut and roll them.

I call these all-rounders, they are a great way to use up any excess clay. They add an extra option to necklaces and bracelets as you can see and don't forget by flattening them you'll have round disc beads as well.

# Project 25. **Burr Walnut**

Turquoise is a cool stone, Burr Walnut is a warm wood. You can add, or substitute cadmium red or viridian to alter the tone. Both add greater depth of colour to the end piece but only add a little and treat as accent colours.

Take equal amounts of black, brown and white. Roll them out and it's almost as if your forming a humbug cane. Keep the layers even and place them on top of one another, roll out gently into a small flat even sheet.

Cut the sheet in half with a long flat blade, do this in a downwards motion so that the cut is even, take care to insure that the amounts are all even because you'll be using them to make a sandwich later on in the process.

# Project 25. **Burr Walnut Cont:**

Hold both halves together, trim if necessary. Using black, brown and white for a second time make a bulls eye cane as shown on page 44 of this book, keep it relatively thick at this stage, cut it in half and place one half to the side.

Take both of the flat humbug pieces that you made earlier, place the bulls eye cane between them and gently close the two halves around it taking care to tuck them completely around the cane, then trim as necessary.

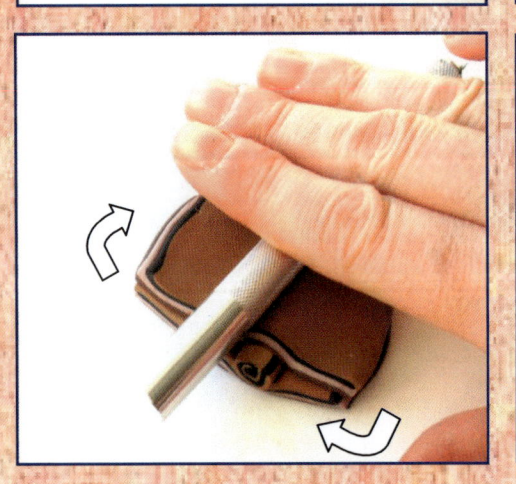

Gently roll with any round handled tool over the entire piece until it becomes flat. Keep turning the piece as you roll it so that the pattern remains crisp. If you continue to roll it in only one direction, the pattern will warp.

# Project 25. Burr Walnut Cont:

When the sheet becomes flat, trim it and cut it for a second time in a downwards motion ensuring that both halves are equal in size. Next roll out a thin layer of orange / red and brown and place on one of the halves

The sides will look like the picture opposite, If they don't, don't worry, walnut like turquoise is natural, no two pieces look the same.
Place the second half of the bulls eye roll in the middle of the two halves.

Roll it again gently in the same way that you did the first time, again it is important to keep turning the piece, as well as flipping it over. This will ensure the patter stays even and doesn't become warped as it levels.

# Project 25. **Burr Walnut Cont:**

You won't notice anything from above but when you turn your Burr Walnut cane to the side it will look like this, once again don't worry if it isn't exactly like this, trees never grow exactly the same way so no pattern is wrong.

Take the cane and even it out as much as possible, then slice it carefully in half again from above so that you have a very long, very narrow, thick cane which from the side will show the incredibly detailed Burr Walnut pattern.

At this stage you can congratulate yourself because you've made your first faux stone and faux wood canes. You have learnt two totally different techniques which can be used on all sorts of stone and wood recipies.

# Project 25. Burr Walnut Cont:

Take some clay in the colour of your choice, roll it until it is around 5mm thick. It should be large enough for you to get two earrings, a pendant, or a bracelet. When you've done this follow the steps for project 16 & 24.

For earrings, set a small hoop of wire, or a hole into each then cook in your oven for at least fifteen minutes at temperature stated. If you are worried about getting two identical shapes make a cardboard template first.

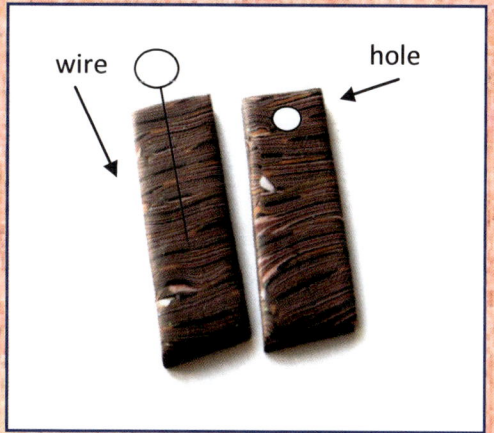

Hint: If you stop the folding process half way through and leave the lines so that they are still quite thick you'll get a lovely agate. If you scrunch it up into a log and slice against the grain you'll get another form of granite.

# Recipe Semi Precious Stones / Kick Start Ingredients Chart

**Black Onyx**
Black (F) finished with Acrylic Glaze
Condition & shape

**Moss Agate**
Metallic Green (F) Black (F)
Translucent (F)
Technique shown on (P76)

**Rhodonite**
Pink Stone Effect (S) Translucent (S)
Technique shown on (P74)

**Topaz**
Orange (S) Translucent (S)  Brown
Stone Effect (S)
Technique shown on (74)

**Goldstone**
Burnt Sienna (F) Cadmium Yellow (F)
Gold Glitter
Add glitter while conditioning

**Unlite**
Orange (F) Pink (F)
Leaf Green (F)
Technique shown on (74)

**Tigers Eye**
Translucent (F) Cadmium yellow (F)
Chocolate (F) Black (F)
Technique shown (P74)

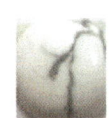

**Howlite**
Translucent (F) Grey (F) Black (F)
Technique shon on (76)

**New Jade**
Translucent (F)
Leaf Green (F)
Acrylic Glaze

**White Agate**
White (F)
Condition & Finish with Acrylic glaze

**Dalmatian Jasper**
Translucent (S)
Black (F)
Technique shown on (74)

**Yellow Turquoise**
White (S)
Ocher (S)
Technique shown on (76)

**Sodalite**
Ultramarne (F) Metallic Blue (F) Black (F) Translucent (F)
Technique shown on (76 )

**Braciated Jasper**
Pillerbox Red (F) Black (F)
Translucent (F)
Technique shown on (P74)

The above chart is designed to start showing you what you can make by mixing various clays using the methods you have just learned. Get a good picture study it and mix up the colours that you see in the stone, set them to the side then chop and slice, you'll soon get the hang of it.
As I said before no stone in nature is ever quite the same in texture, pattern, or colour density.
So in a way you can never really get it wrong.

# Project 26. Easy White Granite

Take some translucent clay, you can experiment with a little black, blue, or pink, Condition the colour through the clay and it will allow you to make different shades of granite but for the moment I'll be sticking to white

The amount of seed beads should be similar to the amount of clay that you are using.
The clay is used as a binder to hold the beads together, you start by pressing down firmly to pick them up.

Condition them through the clay until they almost disappear, don't worry if this happens, just push down on the pile again and repeat the process. The more you add the more they will start to stand out and form the pattern.

# Project 26. **Easy White Granite Cont:**

I have found through some trial and error that the very best clay to use for this particular technique is Sculpey soft. The reason being is that the more you use it the stickier it gets, this makes it pick up the beads far more easily.

Stickiness aside, as you near the end of the process your clay will start to firm out again because of the beads, it will also feel slightly rougher in texture, this is normal and it means that you're doing everything correctly.

Easy granite has a lovely translucent glittery quality to it without all of the fuss of chopping and slicing. Throw in some gold glitter for an extra kick and as I said earlier colour with a slight hint of pink, green, or blue.

# Project 27. Easy Moonstone

Take translucent white again but this time we're adding white rainbow glitter, you can get it in any good craft shop in the card section. Stock up just after Christmas for anything like this because the shops always sell it off cheap.

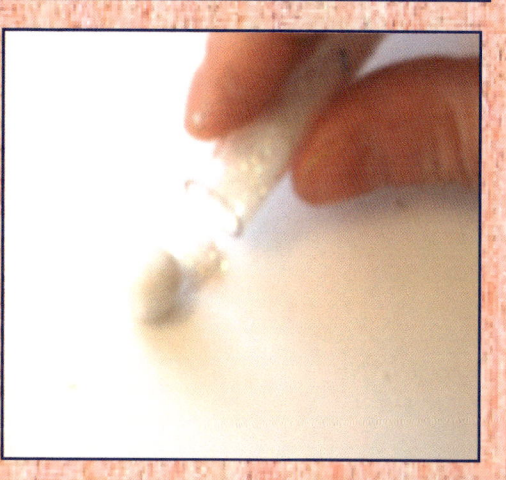

Translucent sculpey is best for this for the same reasons explained in the previous exercise. The amounts are also the same, half clay and half glitter. It sounds a lot but it will soon blend in to become a lovely shiny stone.

You can leave your moonstone white or you can add accent colour in the same way I spoke of in the last section on granit. Don't mix it through thoroughly and always mix it in at the end so that you don't over condition.

# Project 28. **Easy Lava Rock**

This is a great stone to make if you have any old rough black clay lying around. I took this from my scrap jar, if there are any other bit sticking to it leave them on. You will also need rock salt and a little glitter.

Knead the clay thoroughly, mix in a pinch of glitter because if you turn real lava to the light you will see little flecks of colour. Make sure it's mixed through, roll the final piece in the rock salt, equal amounts again.

Cook in your over, take out your lava stone, once it has cooled, drop it in a glass of hot water and leave it for a few hours. During this time the salt will dissolve you will be left with your imitation lava rock.

# Project 29. **Precious Metals**

Pulver comes in a range of standard metallic shades such as old gold, new gold, copper, silver and pewter. It also has a funkier range in metallic blue, green and red. Use it on different coloured clay for different results.

This is an example of some of the shades, the coating on the sculpey translucent white pearls is relatively thick to show the real metallic effect but I have to say that a thinner coating will also give you a freshwater pearl effect.

The picture opposite shows what happens with a heavy dusting of pulvar. The lighter the dusting on translucent clays, the more pearl the effect will be. You should practice this and you'll achieve a range of different beads.

# Project 29. **Precious Metals Cont:**

Pulver comes in a variety of standard metallic shades such as old gold, new gold, copper, silver and pewter. It also has a funkier range in metallic blue, green and red. Use it on different coloured clay for even more results.

This is an example of some of the shades, the coating on the sculpey translucent white pearls is relatively thick to show the real metallic effect. You can seal it with acrylic but only if you want a shiny glazed metallic bead.

The picture opposite shows the difference between a heavy dusting of pulvar 'above' and a lighter dusting in the image opposite.

Hint: Pulvar can also be polished once it has been cooked.

# Project 30. Foils & Leaf

Leaf is great fun, it comes in an envelope that contains thin sheets set between tissue. There are usually ten sheets in a packet and it comes in a variety of finishes. The good thing about it is that it has an ultra shiny finish.

Touch any uncooked clay with your finger, then using the same finger touch the piece of leaf that you want to lift up, you will find that it is so light that it will immediately stick to your finger until it comes into contact with your clay.

As soon as it touches any uncooked clay it will immediately stick to it because this is always stickier than your finger. You can move it around a little but leaf is fragile and if you move it too much it will crack.

# Project 30. **Foils & Leaf Cont:**

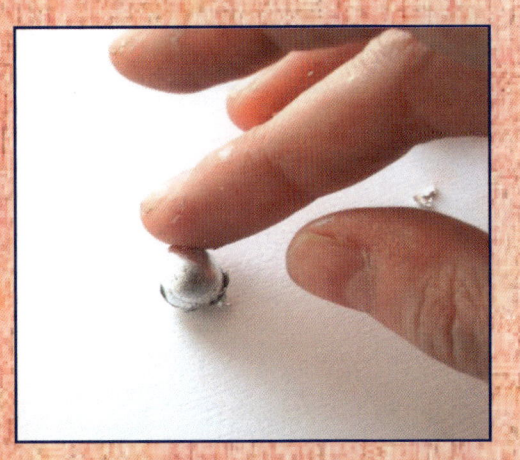

When your clay item is covered press gently and roll it in circles with your finger if it is a bead. If it is a detailed item brush the leaf with a soft paint brush and it will move and fill every little space quite easily.

Any loose leaf should be gathered and either stored in the tissue that it came with, or collected and kept in a jar. Small leaf fragments are great for a wide variety of uses. It is also expensive so don't throw it away unnecessarily.

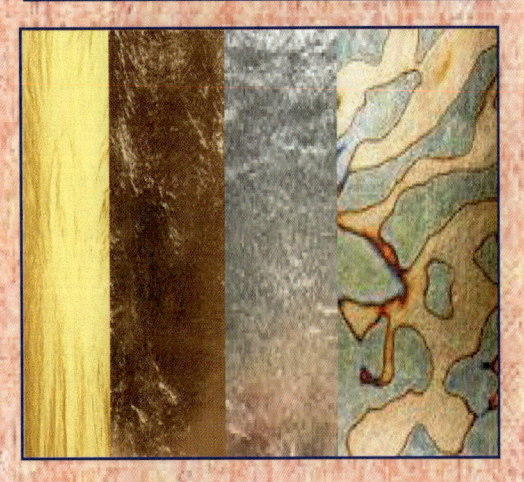

As I said before leaf comes in many formats, gold, old gold, silver, pewter, petrol to name but a few. They should be used sparingly.
Finally for that really special item, real gold leaf can be purchased online.

## CHAPTER SIX

# findings

You can thread your beads and pendants using anything from ribbon, or string to a leather lace once you've popped a hole into them with your pin tool. I use a lot of elastic because it means my bracelets fit more people but really at the end of the day it is always up to you.

The next step after elastic is probably jewelry wire often called fishtail (don't ask me why it's called fish tail, that's one question I can't answer for you, it is a little trickier and you'll need some extra findings.

## Clasp Rings

### Clasps & Rings

Clasps come in a wide range of different shapes and sizes, different metals, different tones, I could go on. The easiest to use are the hook and eye clasp which speaks for itself, however the most secure or at least what people think is the most secure is the bolt ring, I don't think there is much in it if you put them on correctly.

**Lobster Clasp**     **Bolt Ring**     **Toggle Clasp**     **Hook**

## Screw Eyes

### Eye's (Screw eyes)

On the right you will see a set of gold plated screw eyes, they make great hooks and you can get 100 of them for the same price a one jeweler's hook. Aside from the price I think they look much better and they come in a range of metallic effects so you're not just stuck with silver and gold. I feel they are stronger because you screw them into the uncooked clay and you get a firm hold.

## Bails

### Hooked Bail

Bails come in all shapes and sizes; they're used to grab your bead or pendant. once again they work best when applied to uncooked clay because they get a better grip in the raw clay.

They are often very pretty and they are perfect for that special something when you don't want just a hole.

## Bead Caps

### Bead Caps

These are purely decorative, you put one at either side of your polymer clay bead and they give it that extra oomf.

…Aside from this they don't serve any real purpose.

## Brooch Bar

### Brooch Bar

This is the easiest to use, again you push it into the uncooked clay until the holes fill, then push overflow flat so that it overlaps slightly, at this point you can add some liquid sculpey for extra strength but normally you don't need to.

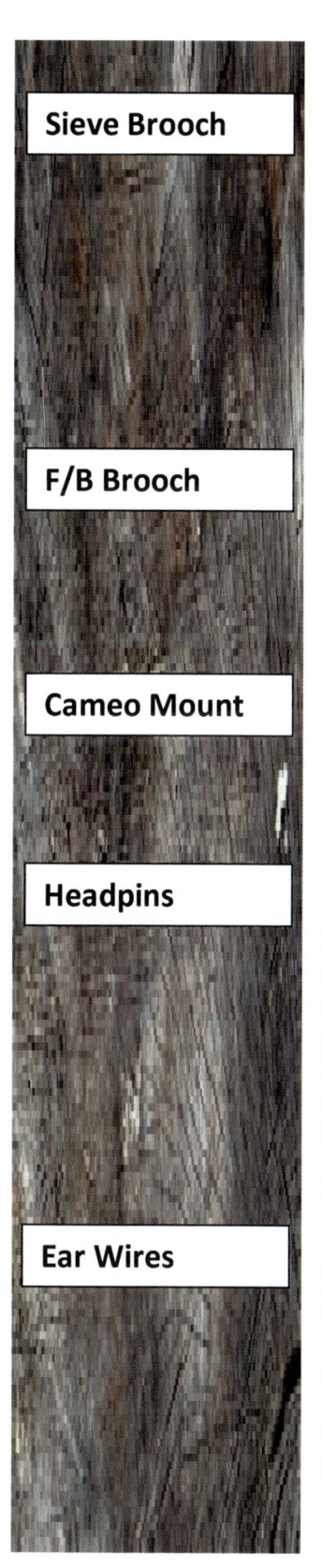

## Sieve Brooch

This is slightly trickier because it comes in two parts but like the bar brooch you push part one (the circle full of holes) against the back of the uncooked clay until it pushes through the holes, even it out gently and cook, then once cooked clip it to the second part

A good thing about the brooch is the fact that if you want to add wired beads you can pop them in the holes as well before cooking.

## Flat Backed Brooch

This is one of the most difficult to use because it has nothing to cling to unlike the other two. I you do use this make sure you add liquid sculpey to the back of it, or press it into the wet clay then remove to leave the indentation. Once cooked add a drop of superglue and push the brooch back on again quickly taking care not to get the glue on your fingers.

## Cameo Mounts

These look lovely sometimes they have a pin but most of the time they have a flat back and you need to add one of the bars I've shown you above in order to make them useful. You can also use them to turn your bead, pendant into a rather nice cabochon which can be used to decorate picture frames, books, belts etc.

## Headpins

Most of the time you use them in the construction of earrings but they are also great for making beads that dangle. If you want to do this you'll need to compliment them with a good pair of long nosed pliers. If you buy a set of long nosed pliers though it will work out cheaper in the end to buy a long roll of wire and make your own head pins.
…And this as they say is the joy of getting involved in a hobby that continually grows.

## …And Finally Ear Wires

I mention these because I strayed into this area of earrings when I spoke about using headpins to make dangly beads.
…But why not have a go, if you make a nice bracelet and a nice necklace who says you won't want a nice pair of earrings to match.

There are of course so many other findings, everything from tiara blanks, to ring blanks, I'm sure you're going to have a blast.

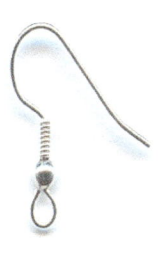

# Glossary of terms

| | | |
|---|---|---|
| A | Acrylic Roller | A clear rod used like a rolling pin for flattening out clay |
| | Achromatic | The white to black colour spectrum |
| | Antiquing | Covering patterned clay in paint and wiping it off |
| | Appliqué | Placing small pieces of clay together to form a larger piece or pattern, appliqué takes its name from quilting |
| B | Baby Oil | Great for your hands and for wiping down cooked clay |
| | Baking | To cook the clay in the oven at the time and temperature set by the manufacturer |
| | Baking surface | The sheet or dish you use especially for cooking your clay and preferably items that are not to be used with food |
| | Ball Stylus | Similar to a needle tool but with a ball end, it is a tool that has its origins in the art of pergiamo |
| | Bead Roller | A special tool that you can buy to create beads that are all exactly the same size and shape |
| | Bolt Ring | A ring attached to a bead or pendant which is used to hold a hook, bolt or catch on a necklace, or bracelet. |
| | Buffing | The act of rubbing uncooked and partially cooked clay with a piece of cling film around your finger, this technique can sometimes remove the need for a glaze |
| | Burning Clay | The act of cooking clay at a higher temperature than the manufacturer has stated |
| C | Cabochon | A domed piece of clay formed by cutting a sphere in half, predominantly used for decoration |
| | Cane | A formed log of clay that carries a design from the beginning of the log to the end like a stick of rock |
| | Cane slice | The term used for the piece taken from a cane, it is sometimes called a tesserae because it is placed in the same way as a mosaic piece |
| | Chromatic | A term used for colour |
| | Clay Blade | A long flat bade used for cutting clay canes, it can be any size |
| | Clay Inlay | To press a pattern into clay, cook it and then press soft clay into the hole and cook again, this technique is similar to marquetry |
| | Clay Stamp | Stamps created for the sole use of impressing patterns into clay |
| | Colour Wheel | A circular diagram that shows primary, secondary and tertiary colours and the way in which they relate to one another |
| | Conditioning | The act of needing the polymers through the clay in order to create a stronger softer clay to work with |
| | Copyright | The act of ensuring no one else can copy your designs |
| | Curing | Similar to baking it makes the clay go hard |
| D | Decorating Chalk | Also called chalk pastels, these can be used to age or embellish |

| | | |
|---|---|---|
| | | uncooked clay |
| E | Extruder | A tool you will find in later books, it is a metal syringe style tool which forces the clay through a series of precut metal die patterns to create long strings of patterned clay |
| F | Faux | The term used for something fake for example faux turquoise |
| G | Glaze | A substance that makes you clay glossy and shiny |
| | Glitter | Small flecks of metal in various grades which can be mixed into uncooked clay to create a sparkle effect |
| I | Image transfer | Copying a printed sheet on to clay using various methods |
| | Inlay | The act of setting small decorations into the clay |
| | Kemper Cutters | Small cutters that are spring loaded to allow ease of use |
| L | Leeching | To place overly soft clay between two sheets of paper in order to remove any excess polymer |
| | Loaf or Log | A term used for a long length of clay |
| | Liquid Polymer Clay | A polymer clay in liquid form, semi translucent it can be used to glue or bond you clay, it can also be used in an image transfer process |
| M | Marbling | Taking two or more colours and blending to achieve a desired effect |
| | Metal Leaf | Commonly called gold leaf, it now comes in many colours, it gives the clay the appearance of a precious metal and it can be used on cooked and uncooked clay |
| | Metallic Powder | Occasionally called Pulvar this can be used in the same way as the leaf, however it is brushed on and only works with uncooked clay |
| | Mica Shift | A technique where layers of clay are placed on top of one another to give the appearance of depth |
| | Mokume Cane | Clay sheets stacked in a tower which when sliced shows a delicate graded pattern |
| | Mold | Made from many materials molds allow the user to create the same pattern / piece again and again instantly |
| P | Pasta Machine | Originally used to make pasta, it can be used to make thin sheets of graduated colour, a rolling pin does the same thing |
| | Paint | Acrylic and thick water colour which can be added to clay at a later stage |
| | Pattern Cutter often called Cookie Cutter | Used to cut continuous shapes from flat sheets of clay |
| | Plasticizer | The substance in clay used to keep it soft |
| | Polymer | The chemical found in your clay which when cured causes it to go hard |
| Q | Quilting Cane | A term used when two or more canes are used to create a broader pattern |
| R | Release Agent | This can be water, oil, or powder depending on the project. |
| S | Sanding | A finishing technique used on partially cooked and cooked clay, it removes minor imperfections |
| | Scrap Clay | Off-cuts that when mixed can be used as a base clay for other projects |
| | Skinner Blend | The technique of creating graduated colour with a pasta machine or roller |
| | Sticky Clay | Clay that is overly soft because it has either too much plasticizer or it has come into contact with a plastic container and is having a reaction. Note the later should be thrown away. |
| T | Translucent | The term used for clay that has clear glass like qualities |

## ABOUT THE AUTHOR

I live with my lovely husband Tom and a big fat cat called Ella, which is short for Cinderella.
I began working with polymer clay in high school but I wasn't very successful with it and I put it aside before heading off to the RSAMD in Glasgow to study stage management and technical theatre.
From there I studied at Glasgow's College of Building and Print, dabbling in photography and ceramics to pay the bills.
Over the years I've had lots of lovely arty jobs, but I eventually ended up back in theatre as a technical teaching assistant before finally settling in Newcastle as a senior demonstration technician in the School of Fashion, Art, Design & Social Sciences, which is a cool title by any standard.
I have been here for fifteen years.

It was no surprise really when in 2009 I got the itch to try something new, I was encouraged to do my Master's degree by an old friend and polymer clay 'which I have to say has never been far from me' wanted its day in the sun, or rather I was told by the interviewing panel that I'd be daft not to do the MA on polymer clay, which until then I'd regarded as light relief, the rest is history.

I thought I knew a lot about it, but in the last few years I've learned so much more, and I realise I'll always be learning.
I have also crashed and burned a lot in order to gain this knowledge.

…And my next step,…well it suddenly hit me why not write books that hopefully teach you without you realising that you're learning and hopefully this is the first of many.

# Evi

Printed in Great Britain
by Amazon